GEORGEHAM
NOW AND THEN

V. A. MEEK

I should like to dedicate this book to Mr Stevenson Balfour who first set me on the local history trail.

Acknowledgements

I should like to thank first of all Meg and Peter Mounteney who passed their file of information on Georgeham into my keeping, gave me permission to use it and offered me great enthusiasm

Thanks are due to Braunton and District Museum and to the North Devon Records Office for their help. Also to Andrew Byrom and Tony Evans for help with the photos.

I should like to thank all those who have encouraged me to write this book, given information and made suggestions.

Many thanks too to my son who volunteered to turn the various bits into book form and deal with the printing.

Introduction

This is an account of Georgeham village and three of the neighbouring hamlets. It is not an account of Georgeham Parish, because Croyde, and several outlying farms have not been included.

However, it is time to make easily available once more the many years' work of Mr Stevenson Balfour, on which I have drawn heavily and to which I have added.

This book has been written with three main purposes in mind:

Firstly it is for those who are interested in the areas they are visiting. The book begins with a look at the village as it is now, with pointers to its past.

Secondly it is for residents who are interested in the development and history of their village.

Thirdly, once readers' interest is aroused, there is a section where some aspects of social and economic local history are looked at in much greater detail.

At the end of the book I have included a Time Line, 500 AD - 2008 for national and local events.

This is followed by a list of sources I have used, and a second list of sources to which I have found references in the course of my researches.

ISBN 978-1-906769-15-4

First Published 2009
Edward Gaskell Publishers
Old Sawmill, Grange Road
Bideford, Devon EX39 4AS

Cover & book design, Front cover photography by Simon Meek

Rear cover photography courtesy the Mounteney collection.

Printed by Lazarus Press,
Unit 7, Caddsdown Business Park,
Bideford, Devon EX39 3DX

Contents

GEORGEHAM.
ROCK HILL
THE GLEBE
DAVIDS HILL
P.
1.
2.
3.
4.
5.
6.
7.
8.
9.
11a
11.
12.
13
14.
15.
16
17.
18.
19.
20.
21.
22.
23.
24.
26.
27.
28.
29.

Georgeham Now

A Walk round the village.

It seems a good idea to look first at the village as it is today - to take a walk round the main village, starting as you arrive in the village from Croyde.

Mr Gammon senior, blacksmith, watched by three young Londoners, c. 1906

1. On the right is The Forge House. The main part of the building was indeed a forge, with a working blacksmith, Mr Gammon. As a child I loved to go and poke my nose over his half door and watch him blow up the fire, heat lumps of iron and then hammer them into horse shoes, bits to mend farm machinery, or whatever was needed. This must have been about 1945. Some farms were still using horses so I was also able to watch him clamp the shoes on, hissing, and smell the burning hoof as it bedded in. He also put iron rims on wheels, placing them on the stone former which is still visible on the verge outside the house, and throwing buckets of water at them to cool them quickly.

At the top of the steps, where swallows love nesting was a tiny flat. Lois Lamplugh, who wrote about her life here, records that her family lived there for a while. (A Book of Georgeham and the North West Corner of Devon)

2. On the left is the Village Hall, or Institute as it was called. It was built at the expense of the family then at Pickwell, the Elliotts, whose initials it bears, on land given by Mr Lock and was designed to provide a centre of social life as an alternative to the pubs. This was not all together successful, but the hall has been well used. A youth club was based there. There was and is a skittle alley. Dances on Saturday nights were a great feature, still fondly remembered. Best of all, at intervals a van would arrive with miles of cables, mysterious machines and a screen. That night there was a film show, black and white, rather sparky and crackly, but fun.

The Village Hall is still well used by clubs, by the school, for talks, by the W I, for parties and functions of all sorts.

The sundial on the front shows local time, about 20 minutes later than standard GMT.

Collecting drinking water from the pump outside The Haven

Inside there are two rather beautiful works of calligraphy, made for a friend of the Elliotts, Miss Kemp-Welch, who also painted the reredos in the church. The panels give a history of the village.

3. Turn down to your left, down Netherham Hill. On the right is a curious set of steps going nowhere. This was a mounting block belonging to the old and much altered cottage behind it.

In the early 1940s Mr Physick lived here and, with his horse and cart, collected refuse from the village. His grey horse, Tom, lived in the orchard below the house.

4. Across the stream, there was, until about 1952, a pump which supplied drinking water to those houses at this end of the village without their own well. Mains water arrived at this time.

5. On the right, on the far side of a back lane there are some renovated buildings which started life as piggeries and then degenerated into stores. Some are now converted into holiday accommodation.

Georgeham 1932, land at the back of Speedwell

The three cottages at the end of this back lane, in the 19th century, belonged to the village, serving as "poor houses".

In the 1950s the village long net could be found drying here.

6. From a restored first floor barn opposite the lane I have a horn cider beaker which the builder found and gave me. The horn had been straightened, by steaming, and has a wooden bung to make the bottom. This barn was the site of a cider press belonging to West End Farm.

7. On the corner on the left, the house called West End was West End Farm, and before that the Ring o'Bells pub, belonging to a gentleman called Scamp.

8. From the top of Netherham Hill, you can see the school to the left, built in 1868, with what was the school house for the Head conveniently built on to it. The school has strong links with St George's Church and has been central to village life since it was built. People often say, 'Five generations of my family have been through that school.'

Turn right here, into Church Road.

9. On the left are what are sometimes called the oldest cottages in the village, with a 14th century date suggested. They have been well restored.

10. On the right is The Barn, which had the reputation in the 1930s of housing a nudist colony. Two elderly gentlemen, gossiping at the barber's in Braunton one day, cheerfully remembered cycling over to Georgeham, and climbing up the church tower to view this sight. The elderly lady, Miss Johnson, who lived there used to walk weekly into Barnstaple to do her shopping.

11. A little further and on the left you will find a wonderful rock ledge, one of many reminders that Georgeham is built on rocky terraces above a stream.

12. Facing you along the road is Crowberry Cottage, which bears a blue plaque showing that the author, Henry Williamson lived there for a while. Attached to it and called, as it was by Williamson, Billy Goldworthy's Barn, is a well restored barn, which, for years presented big black wooden doors on which were placed flyers for circuses and other events. It is claimed it was used for dances during the Ham Revel.

13. Foote Farm, on the right dates from 1630. Until recently the farm's cows used to wander through the village as they came home for milking.

14. The bridge over the stream, next to the farm, bears a plaque, now very difficult to read, showing that it was built by two gentlemen from the village in 1868, Richard Pearse and Robert Scamp.

15. On the opposite side of the road is the most famous house in the village, Skirr Cottage, central to Williamson's writing about the village and where he started "Tarka the Otter".

16. Continuing along Church Road, just as you begin to go up the hill, Chertsey Cottage was previously a shop and the village post office (one of three places which have housed the post office). Another of the cottages here was a dame school for a while in the 1900s.

Foote Farm

Next is the pub, for years called The King's Arms, but now bearing the name Williamson gave it in his books, The Lower House.

17. On the left, as you go up the hill is the lych gate to the church, by which the dead enter the churchyard. Coffins rest here briefly and are met by the priest.

The Lych Gate

18. Millies Cottage on the corner was once a brewhouse for the ales the church sold to defray expenses before the Reformation. It became a pub, The Victoria Inn, later a cottage. During restoration a Bodley grate was found there, and behind that two cloam bread ovens, one behind the other. The first was glazed brown and yellow, the one behind lined with coarse stoneware. Look across the main road at the old stone barns which were also church property.

19. Just next to Millies Cottage is a little stone building, currently used as a store by the church. It was originally the death house or mortuary, where bodies could be kept before burial.

Chapel Street, looking towards the Kings Arms, 1934. At this time there was a stone built shed in front of what is now called Joby's. Joby Thomas was a carpenter.

20. Before going any further, turn back and complete the circuit of the main village. There are two old cottages here, First is Joby's. Joby was the village carpenter, his workshop is now part of the pub. An old photo shows low buildings in front of the cottage. Next is Rosemary Cottage, formerly Rose Cottage. Here during the war, lived Granfer Brown, the bottoms of his trousers tied firmly with string - to keep the rats out I was told!

21. The village shop and post office was once a bakers, but in the 1940s and 50s was one of the two main shops in the village, the post office migrating between them. It sold everything and smelled wonderfully of the paraffin kept in a large container in the back of the shop.

22. Next is a little row of cottages. Coral Cottage at least was thatched until 1972. Here, in the 1940s lived a gentleman who sold vegetables. As a young man, his profession was given, in deeds in my possession, as 'rabbit trapper'.

The old bee boles at Gwynant

Georgeham Village shop and Post Office, c. 1900 and 2008

23. The two next houses are relatively new. The blacksmith lived in the first of them. In the wall between these two houses are some holes which were made to take the old straw bee hives and are called “bee boles”. These bee hives belonged to Mr G, who lived in a house which no longer exists. He gained fame by knifing P C Creech in 1883, who died because of the attack - the only known murder in the village.

24. After three more cottages you come to the “new” Baptist Chapel, built in 1883.

The Baptist Chapel

Two doors beyond that was the original chapel. Built in 1837 by the Methodists, transferred to the Baptists, it became too small and was converted first into the minister's house - hence "Manse". The minister however moved to a larger building at Cross. So the old chapel became "The Old Manse".

This completes the circuit of the main village, so retrace your steps, back to the shop, past the "Lower House" and you come again to the church.

25. In front of the church is an area of old cobbles forming a pavement and gutter. It is said that these were part of an area used for the "Ham Revel", with dancing on the cobbles.

26. A brief history of the church is in the later "Georgeham Then" section. For the casual visitor, the most obvious thing about it is the tall, sturdy tower, which dominates the village. It is just high enough for the sea to be visible from the top. It was built in the 14th century and its height may be due to its use as a lookout for the assorted pirates, Scots, French, Turkish, Algerian, who took Lundy between the 14th and 17th centuries. The tower houses a peel of eight bells as visitors in the village on Sunday mornings, or practice night, will soon notice.

Opposite the church, the grey stone buildings now converted to living accommodation. were barns belonging to the church.

27. Continuing a bit further. St George's House was the rectory. A beautiful old house, built in 1880s on the site of the earlier rectory. The stream runs close to the house, and occasionally, in rare times of flood, through it.

28. Opposite , the road runs up Rock Hill. At the bottom, the house was at one time a general store and post office and also a butcher's who hung his

Artie Thomas' shop at the bottom of Rock Hill, c. 1940, and today.

Rock Hill, Georgeham in the 1930s (inset 2008). This was a row of individual homes, some very small.

meat in an old barn to the left.

29. Next comes The Rock Inn, well known to visitors. It turns up in Henry Williamson's books about the village as "The Upper House", one of his haunts where he used to sit and yarn with his friends and the villagers he wrote about so vividly. The pub was enlarged when two neighbouring cottages, Rock Home and Jubilee were bought for this purpose.

The Rock Inn 2008

Further up some very old, small cottages have been restored and often combined. Curiously, these cottages had their 'conveniences' , sheds, or possibly piggeries, on the opposite side of the road. Originally, however, the road ran along the backs of the houses, a track which is still there.

So far, most of the buildings mentioned were in place by 1850. Since then there have been various developments. In the 1930s, on Newberry Road, ten 'council houses' were built. At a similar time several bungalows appeared, especially on the road to Putsborough. According to Henry Williamson these were built to prevent part of the fields behind them becoming a new cemetery, a wonderful saga, well worth reading. It was published as "A Democratic Story", in "Tales of a Devon Village", and again in "The Village Book".

Longlands Lane was developed in the 1950s, land behind being bought as a recreation ground for use by the whole village. Currently it houses a football pitch and a play area for young children. There are plans to make more use of it.

Putsborough Close was the next development. Davids Hill was built in 1979, a major development. Then Williamson Close by the Village Hall. Finally, the Glebe Field, which had been sold many years previously, was developed in 2002, This development included a village green and a much needed car park, which is particularly necessary when weddings and funerals take place at the church.

Around the village there are several farms and hamlets, North and South Hole Farms, Crowborough Farm, Incledon Farm, North Buckland, Darracott, Pickwell, Forda, Cross, Putsborough. Croyde is the other main centre. These, along with part of Spreacombe and part of Heddon Mill form the Parish of Georgeham.

Georgeham then

1

We know that people have been in the area since Mesolithic times (8000 - 3000 BC) because many flint artefacts have been found. Flint does not occur in the area. Either people went to fetch it or it was traded in. At the beginning of this period sea levels were much lower, marshes stretching across to Wales with the river Severn running down the middle. A few artefacts have been found which may date from the Bronze Age. There are two standing stones, both on private land. One of them, at North Buckland, lying prone as long as anyone can remember, has recently been stood upright. These stones gave rise to the legend of the Pickwell giant who stood up at Pickwell where one stone remains and hurled one inland and another out to sea.

There is nothing obvious here from the Iron Age, although there is a 'settlement' at Spreacombe, nor the Roman period except perhaps the odd coin and nothing that we know of from the so called Dark Ages. Braunton however has a church dedicated to the Celtic saint, St Brannock who appears to have settled there after an adventurous life, in the sixth century. That the church retained its Celtic dedication suggests that a community continued to live there after the arrival of the Saxons, communicated with them and either lived side by side with the newcomers or was at least partially integrated with them. Braunton's river has also kept its Celtic name, Cam, though it has been rationalised to Caen. It is likely therefore that there was a significant pre Saxon presence in the area generally. Whether they were well spread out, had been affected by the fifth century 'plague', or simply moved to Cornwall or Wales or even Brittany is unknown. It is suggested that fields and places called 'Yelland' were recognised by the Saxons as being abandoned farmland. We have one such field in the parish.

2

The Saxons reached here in the seventh century, probably by the land route along the north of Exmoor. They were looking for land to farm by then and mostly settled in individual farmsteads, except in Braunton, a Saxon royal manor, where a village was created and the fertile Great Field farmed communally. We know little about the Saxons who first came here. The various kingdoms fought among themselves. The dialect use of 'us' for 'we' suggests they may have been Mercian rather than West Saxon since this form is found in manuscripts from Mercia. In the end, Devon was part of the West Saxon kingdom.

Here they founded a settlement, called simply "Ham" at the head of a valley whose small stream flows down to Croyde. Where exactly? Well, they were Christians, close to Braunton which had been a centre for Christianity well before the Saxons made it a minster, and which King Edgar had bought back from Glastonbury Abbey. King Edgar liked settlements to have at least a chapel. According to Charles Croslegh , writing about Bradninch, these chapels were often on slightly higher ground, so people could look up to them. This would suggest that the first settlement was down the hill from the church, on the other side of the stream and probably a bit above stream level. There was once a very old farm complex in this area, opposite Foote Farm. In the 18th century it was called Crowberry. Farmer Smith later moved to the farm now called Crowberry above Newberry Cottages. The cottage built on the old site was still called Crowberry in the 1839 Tithe Apportionment.

Of the Viking attacks in this area, in the 9th century we know little, though they had a base on Lundy and attacked the Taw estuary in 851.

By the end of the 10th century the Saxons had organised the area as part of the Braunton Hundred and into townships or vils which contained several holdings or tythings, later manors. At the beginning of the 14th century, the manors. Georgeham, Pickwell and Woolacombe formed one township; Croyde, East Lobb, Saunton and Blakewell Pyne formed another. Not much is known about the area at the end of the 10th century when England had Danish rulers (Canute). Canute kept the south-west in his own care; earldoms existed elsewhere, in Kent, Mercia and Northumberland. Possibly the name of the pre Conquest owner of Pickwell, one Ulf, is a trace of this period. Canute's sister was married to a Dane called Ulf (not, probably, the same man) who was at one point regent of Denmark.

The Danes were Christian by this time and they seem to have changed little in the way England was run, continuing the Saxon laws and organisation.

3

By the eleventh century nearly all the current farms, hamlets and villages existed. We learn from the Domesday Book that they did not however all belong to the same person either before or after 1066.

William I gave Pickwell to Mowbray, Bishop of Coutances as part of his huge holding, while Georgeham (Ham), Hole, Spreacombe and Saunton went to Theobald Fitz Berners (often referred to asTetbald).

(The final "Exchequer" version of the Domesday Book was compiled from regional records - in the case of Devon, the Exeter Domesday Book. The scribe sometimes misread the "P" of the Exeter version as a "W". This occurred in the case of Pilton and also Pilland.

The name of Pickwell was rendered unrecognisable as Wedicheswelle; Pedicheswelle in the Exeter version. The Pickwell entry was identified only after the manuscript in the Village Hall had been made.

Picaltone has been identified as Bickleton. (This information is from the 1985 revision of the translation of the Domesday Book, pub. Phillimore.)

Some photos of Georgeham Village Hall show a tall sign bearing a picture of a Saxon and his dog. This represents Edmar/Etmar who held, along with much other land, the small manors of Georgeham and Hole before the Norman Conquest.

From the 12th century we hear of people called after the places where they lived - there were the 'de Holes', the 'de Pidkervilles, 'de Santons' at Saunton and a Galfride de Ham'.

Between 1231 and 1252 we have the first reference of "Ham St George'. Before that it was simply Hamme or Ham, probably meaning "the settlement". It is possible that a church, dedicated to St. George had been founded here or that the existing church had been rededicated. St George was a favoured saint of the Crusaders. Perhaps one of the de St Aubin family had been to the

Crusades.

By the end of the 13th century the Georgeham, Hole and Pickwell manors were part of the lands of this family.

More detailed information about the area in these early centuries can be found in a later section - "Landholding"

In 1261 during the lordship of the third Sir Mauger de St Aubin, George-ham was separated from Braunton as a parish by - "the consolidation of the vicarage of that chapel with the parsonage" (Reichel). The tithes from then on were paid to the Rector of Georgeham, the first of whom was Oliver de Tracy. He also claimed the tithes from Croyde, but they had been previously paid to the Priory of St Mary Magdelene in Barnstaple. It was agreed to pay 40s per year in lieu of the tithes. In 1307 the then Rector, Edmund de Knoyle, tried again. He and 17 locals descended on Croyde, found the tithe goods and brought them up to Georgeham!. This cost the Rector £10 in a fine, and the 17 men £10 in damages. However, in 1311 all the tithes from the parish were judged to belong to Georgeham, although £5 was paid annually to the Priory until its dissolution.

The third Mauger de St Aubin (there were, it seems, four) was also for a time Constable of Lundy. He fought in the Welsh wars and must have been a per-son of considerable importance holding other lands along the North Devon coast. Wealthy too. He lent 100 silver marks to the bishop. He is said to be the knight whose effigy is in Georgeham church.

Pickwell, Georgeham, Hole, and eventually North Buckland continued to be closely linked,; the manors being split or combined by marriage and inherit-ance, or occasionally by purchase, until the 20th century. Croyde however, and Putsborough were never part of this grouping.

By this time sheep were being farmed in considerable numbers in the area, and cloth woven for home use and export. There were several fulling/tucking mills. In 1303 a merchant guild was set up in Barnstaple concerned with every aspect of the wool trade. Cloth was one of the cargoes shipped out of Barn-staple. However, we have no record of Georgeham's involvement in this trade.

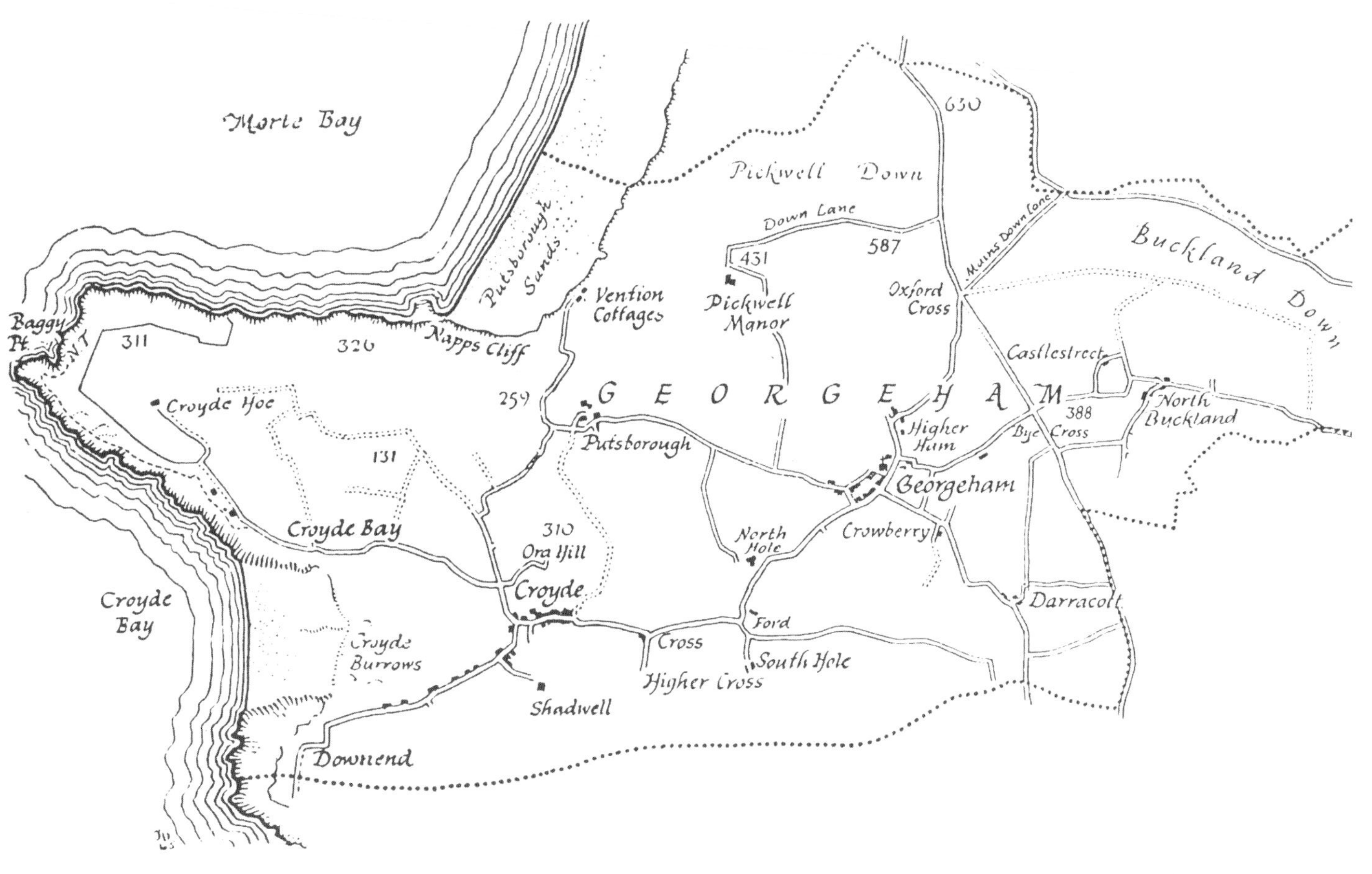

Georgeham Parish

4

In the beginning of 14th century the area must have been quite prosperous. Sir Mauger died in 1294. His tomb was presumably placed in the church reasonably soon after his death, so the church must have been stone built by then. The high tower also dates from the 14th century.

According to the records of Bishop Grandisson, at the end of this century and the beginning of the next, private chapels were licensed at Croyde, Spreacombe, North Buckland, Hole and Pickwell. It does not necessarily follow that these were new buildings. It is possible that some chapels existed before the parish was consolidated and St George's became the parish church.

In 1332, the Devon Lay Subsidy also records Mauger and Walter atte Ford, as well as some well known local names, Arnolf Fot (Foot) and Walter Brown. (More details can be found in the section "Inhabitants")

We have no references to the plague affecting the village - perhaps it was lucky.

Meanwhile, the big holdings had begun to be split up and were increasingly farmed by free tenants who paid rent rather than providing labour. Yeoman farmers had appeared. In Henry III's time Hole had been handed over to Gilbert de Hole. It had various owners until, in 1519, it was bought by Sir Thomas Dennys.

Apparently a family farming at least ten acres could live securely. Less than that left farmers vulnerable to drought, rain, and disease of both crops and cattle.

Everyone paid tithes, usually in kind, to the church, which also owned some farm land (Glebe).

....

We have little information about the area in the 15th Century. Life presumably went on as usual while the rest of the country experienced the Wars of the Roses. There must be information somewhere, but the only information

I have is that in 1458 Georgeham paid 11d towards the cost of the bridge at Barnstaple!

There seems, however, to have been major changes to the church, with the south aisle added at this time, a large window at each end. The window at the east end was subsequently blocked up when the Pickwell chapel was created.

This century saw the wool trade out of Barnstaple at its height, exporting good cloth.

Cattle or sheep were kept in small fields which meant that they didn't need constant watching. Some farmers in North Devon had summer grazing rights on Exmoor.

5

However, on the information front, things change in the 16th century. In 1509 Henry VIII came to the throne and in 1538 parishes were required to keep registers. Those from Georgeham are complete. The earliest were on paper, but copied on to parchment in 1597.Amongst other things they tell us that when plague reached the village Joan Heddon was the last person to die from it, in 1571. Twenty-seven people had died. In 1n 1680 Halleys Comet was "visible to us heer"; 1651 shows the baptism of the son of Richard Clarke who was married to his former wife's sister. In 1696 the baptism is recorded of Francis Perryman, born in 1694 in Newfoundland. Ursula Tooker, widow, died in 1683 at the grand age of 98.

Sadly, "Creech, Walter John, died 7th September 1883, aged 9 months"; the little son of the murdered policeman.

....

In 1569 Queen Elizabeth I was concerned about a possible Spanish invasion, and lists were drawn up, headed by the most important person in the parish, of what had to be provided in terms of men and arms. In our case, John Newcourt from Pickwell headed the list. The poorer people had to contribute to 2 corselets, 2 pikes, 2 calivers, and 2 murrions. The "able men" included 10 archers, 4 harquebusiers, 9 pikemen and 2 billmen (sic).

....

One of Elizabeth's first moves on becoming queen was to state her supremacy over all, including ecclesiastical matters, in this country.

In "Selected Statutes and other Constitutional Documents", edited by G Prothero, and quoted by Julia Pickard in "Elizabethan London", we learn that in 1559 Elizabeth issued injunctions that all shrines and paintings in churches had to be destroyed, and that a "Comely and honest pulpit" should be provided in every parish. All images shrines, tabernacles, rood lofts and monuments of idolatry had to be removed or defaced; walls had to be whitewashed. The Ten Commandments was to be inscribed on the wall in a prominent place. Church bells, however, were allowed to remain. Coloured glass windows could be retained on the understanding that they would be replaced eventually by plain glass.

Furthermore, church attendance was compulsory. Absence could be viewed as treason.

This all sounds very draconian, but Elizabeth was trying to achieve stability and uniformity, and treading a difficult line between Roman Catholicism and extreme Protestantism.

It seems therefore that it was at this time, the second half of the 16th century, that the Rood loft disappeared, the carving (now in the chancel) hidden behind the blocked-up door which had led to the Rood loft and the piscinas disguised behind plaster; all to be found again during the 1876 restoration.

Instructions on how parishes should deal with their Poor also date from Elizabeth's reign and remained in force until 1834. *(Lisa Pickard, "Elizabethan London")*

With the West Country providing many ships for war and exploration, some using Ilfracombe and Bideford, there was a great demand for supplies of all sorts. This must have given a considerable boost to local agriculture.

It seems that the village was quite prosperous by the 17th century. The population continued to grow. In 1641, in the Protestation Returns (people were required to "vow and protest" that they would follow the protestant religion, defend the king and preserve the Union): from Georgeham 211 people signed, all men, so there were probably more than 600 people in the parish.

In 1660 four collections were made ; 23 shillings for those suffering from a fire at Fremington; 6 shillings and 8 pence for rebuilding the quay at Combwich; the same for rebuilding the quay at Watchet; 3 shillings and 4 pence to help Milton Abbas. Later there were collections to help with problems in Marlborough and Kingston upon Thames.

Houses were being built or rebuilt. Foote Farm dates from 1631; Millies cottage bears the date of 1678 - surely a makeover as it had been the old church brewhouse.

....

The Civil War does not appear to have affected Georgeham, although men went from Braunton for training at Torrington. There was, however, a change of rector both at the beginning and the end of the Commonwealth.

....

The first map (See colour section) showing the village was published about 1675, by Mr Ogilby - a much reproduced strip map, often found framed on hotel walls. This map, of which there are several versions shows the "post route" from Ilfracombe to Torrington. The route follows what is now a footpath down through Spreacombe, through Georgeham down to Forda and then by the footpath Hole Lane to the top of Saunton Down, down Hannaburrow Lane and then out to Crow Point at the end of Saunton beach, across the river etc. This route which was marked on the 1809 OS map, was used by sailors in the 20th century commuting between Ilfracombe and Bideford. It remains, in the parish as a bridleway.

Another interesting path is footpath no. 1, which leads from Church Road, up a lane, then across two fields until it joins the Pickwell Road. This path comes

Part of Pickwell Estate map 1833

and goes on the old maps, sometimes leaving only the lane and a path across one of the fields.

On the 1833, Pickwell estate map, no direct route exists between Pickwell and Georgeham although part of the path is shown. It is possible that footpath no.1 was a very old link between the dwellings at Pickwell and St. George's Church, a 'coffin road' perhaps.

6

In the 18th century the church was "beautified" as they wrote proudly on the wall. We have little information about an earlier church building but in 1967 half of a 13th century font was found in the churchyard, datable because it still had one of the staples enabling it to be locked. In the 1876 restoration some remains of a possible north aisle were found and fragments of an ancient tiled floor. A stone carving and two piscinas were also found and are now in the church. The stone effigy of Mauger de St Aubin was, according to Westcote in the 17th century, accompanied by one of his wife.

When the church was "beautified" in 1762 it was given a gallery, a "rich stucco ceiling", box pews and a generally Georgian appearance with round-topped sash windows. By 1771 there was no sign of Sir Mauger's wife's effigy, and his own had been moved. We have a photo of this church, taken before the next restoration in 1876.

Interior of Georgeham Church before the 19th century restoration

It is interesting that five bells were cast for the church in 1748, another cast or recast in 1765, so plans for the "beautification" must have been long standing.

The rector in 1714 recorded the making and casting of the church bells. This may have been done on site, which was quite common at the time.

The Church Terrier, below, stated that in 1727 there were six bells. In 1748 the bells were cast in Gloucester. These bells carried the inscriptions they still have today. Three of them bear what look to be copies of much earlier inscriptions:

> "In concord such they please as much"
> "As we that cheer the listening ear"
> "Let men agree as well as we"

The other bells carry the names of their donors.

The inscriptions, given in a letter from 1926 when the bells were inspected and two more added, read:

Treble: Let men agree as well as we. A R 1748 (AR was the bell founder)
2nd: Mr John Richards, Gent. Ch. Warden. TR 1765 (Thomas, son)
3rd: In concord such They'll please as much. AR 1748
4th: As we that cheer the listening ear. AR 1748
5th: Mr William Chichester and Mr Jn. Richards.
We were all cast in Gloucester by Abel Rudall. 1748
Tenor: The Rev. W. Chichester, Rect. - John Harris, Esq. AR 1748

....

There is a very thorough "Armory of Georgeham Church" by H. Stevenson Balfour in Transactions of the Devonshire Association, vol 101, which includes information by T. Westcote from his visit in 1653.

....

Information about the village increases vastly in the 18th century. From 1727 we have a "Terrier", a list of church land, houses, barns and tithes, which gives us the names of the fields and owners of neighbouring ones. It makes interesting reading. Here is a slightly simplified version of it:

A list of those houses, land and tithes which belong to the Rectory of Georgeham, made in 1727.

A house built of and roofed with stone, containing a hall with earth floor and wood panelled walls; a parlour with a wooden floor and wood panelled walls; a small parlour with a wooden floor; dining room; kitchen with stone floor; dairy; pantry; three cellars; brew house; seven bedrooms, three with wall hangings, three with plain white walls; a study and a closet.
The outhouses have stone and cob walls and are thatched. There are two barns, one near the house and a larger one in Croyde. There are two stables, a shippen, hay store and dove house.

The glebe (church) lands are 33 acres and enclosed, namely;

- the barn Close, about 3.5 acres bounded by the manor lands and Highways.
- the Winnard Hill, 1.5 acres, bounded by lands of the Manor, of John Harris Esq. And the lands of Wright and Deane.
- Five Acres, about 7.75 acres, bounded by the lands of John Harris Esq. , Wright and Hoblin.
- the Pitis, 4 acres, bounded by the lands of the Manor and of John Harris Esq.
- Stone Park, 2 acres, half bounded by the lands of the Manor and of Deane.
- Higher East Field, about 7 acres, half bounded by the Manor lands.
- Lower East Field, about 6 acres, bounded by lands of thee Manor and of Wright and Deane.
- the Bye Cross Meadow, about 2 acres, bounded by the lands of the Manor and of Chichester and Wood.
- the Butt Close, about .33 acre, bounded by lands of the manor and of Wright and Deane.
- the Home Stall which consists of two little orchards, about .25 acre each, and two gardens, all bounded by the lands of Wright.

There are 23 young ash and elm trees growing in the churchyard (felled, diseased in 1970s).

Monies paid out - £5 to poor clergymen's widows of Newton Bushall; £1 to the Dean of Exeter; 2s 6d to the Lord of the Manor; 1s 6d to Mr Hoblin.

Monies received - 2d for an offering; 1s for a marriage; 6d for Churching; burials are free, but mortuary fees are paid.

Tithes are paid in kind of varying sorts, although the Manor mill pays 2s 4d and the other two mills pay 2s each. 1s is paid for a cottage, 6d for a calf, id for the milk of a cow, a farthing for the milk of a ewe, 1d for a herb garden.

The church owns two large Bibles, two books of Common Prayer, a Book of Homilies, a surplice, a stone font, a Communion Table, a carpet, a linen table cloth, a Communion cup and cover, weighing 2.5 ounces, engraved with Richard's Arms, a silver patten weighing 11.5 ounces, a pewter plate, two pewter flagons, a pulpit cushion, a bier and a black hearse cloth, six bells.

The Rector repairs the Chancel, the parish the rest of the church and the churchyard fences, except the hedge which is repaired by the adjoining property.
The Clerk's salary is 16s, the Sexton's 8s. Both officers are paid by the Rector.

This document was signed by 24 parishioners including two churchwardens and two Overseers.

....

There were problems in 1746/7 when twenty people died of a "violent pleurotic plague".

....

In 1755, Revd. Jeremiah Milles or Miles, Precentor and later Dean of Exeter Cathedral sent a questionnaire to all the parishes in the diocese. The one for Georgeham was completed, not by the rector but by a schoolmaster from Barnstaple. It tells us that "Ham Town was in the middle of it (parish); the villages of Putsborough, Croyde and Cross to the west, and Darracott to the `east. George Buck, Esq., was lord of the manor of Ham and (North) Buckland; the manor was dismembered among John Harris, Esq., Philip Webber, Gent. (Buckland) and Messrs Joseph Baller and Smith, Esq. The church was in Mr Buck's manor and in the middle of the parish. The tower was 70 feet high and had 6 bells. ...." There was a gentleman's seat at Pickwell owned by John Harris and a ruined chapel at Croyde. On St George's Day there was the Ham Revel. About 100 hogsheads of cider were produced from 30 acres of orchards. Cattle were black and "handsome all".

....

In 1765 Benjamin Donn produced a map showing the seats of local gentlemen. Pickwell was the seat of John Harris, Esq.

From an 18th century manuscript (a diary kept by Philip Webber of Buckland), we learn that at that time, in the highway between Georgeham and Croyde, at Cross there was still the base of an old cross, presumably a preaching cross predating the church.

Apart from Dean Milles' questionnaire we know that land and money was made available to set up two little schools, one in Georgeham, one in Croyde. This was organised by the Revd Thomas Hole who became rector in 1783. His family were rectors here until 1914. The last one was a hunting man and kept his hounds in a barn in what is still known as Kennelfield.

John Harris, mentioned above, was elected MP for Barnstaple in 1741 and 1754. Along with Mr Webber of Buckland and the Chichesters who had land in the area he was a member of Barnstaple Turnpike Trust. It was realised at this time that the old narrow tracks were unsuitable for commercial transport. Most were unusable by carts and most transport in the area used pack ponies who had a reputation for hurtling down the hills to the danger of any pedestrian.

....

At the end of the century there was the excitement of the Napoleonic War. Invasion was expected, plans drawn up to evacuate the population inland - across country, not blocking up the roads which might be needed by the military! A watch was kept on the coast and ships occasionally sighted. Agriculture flourished supplying the ships and military centres.

New barns seem to have been built at this time. The 1809 OS map shows barns just off Long Lane, called Hole Barns. They disappeared before the 1839 Tithe map was made,. However, the western end of Long Lane, where it widens before meeting the bridleway, is paved with large flat stones, quite unlike the rest of the track. It would have made an excellent turning or loading area.

Surveying for the first OS map was done at the end of the century, originally for military purposes, under the control of Colonel Mudge. This map was the basis for all OS maps of the area until the second edition (usually dated 1904) contour information and then railways added later. The only local road not on this map is the Braunton - Croyde road through Saunton. This road was built in 1906.

In 1794/5 HMS Weazle was wrecked off Baggy Point, perhaps the most famous of the many wrecks. Mr Webber of Buckland kept a diary, which mentions many wrecks on Saunton, Croyde, Barnstaple Bar, Baggy and Morte Points and his difficulties in keeping the remains out of the clutches of the locals. From the Weazle however up to 100 men were lost, some recovered and buried at Georgeham, Braunton and Mortehoe. The sale of the wreckage is recorded in detail, £6 6s being paid for the mainmast. Part of the foremast was bought by the Rev. Hole.

One of the small houses in the village, built around this time, has part of a mast as its main beam supporting the upper floor!

A carving from HMS Weazle can still be seen on a house in Putsborough.

....

Carving from HMS Weazle.

From 1799 we have the list of the Georgeham Volunteers, a wonderful collection of local names. There is a similar list of the 1944 Home Guard. Both lists can be found in the later "Inhabitants" section.

We also have a copy of the 1791 and 1832 Land Tax Assessment lists. The Land Tax Act granted aid to His Majesty King George III; in 1832, posthumously.

On both occasions the money raised from Georgeham was £223 12s.

These lists subsequently formed the basis for deciding who could vote; any male whose land was valued at £2 or more.

7

The prosperity did not continue long into the 19th century. The war ended; there was less demand for produce and the wool trade was in decline. Even in 1739 wool was being imported from Ireland for export from Barnstaple. By 1853 people were giving up, emigrating to America (ships sailed from Bideford) or moving to other parts of the country and the growing industrial centres.

Pickwell no longer had a resident owner; it became a tenanted farm and this was the pattern for North Buckland too, meaning that there was no longer an important landowner living locally. This situation continued until the end of the century when it became fashionable to buy large rural houses and take part in local affairs.

....

About this time non-conformist preachers were inspiring people in the parish. There were Methodists, then Baptists in Croyde. Their first chapel was built in 1817. A small chapel was built in Georgeham in 1837 for the Methodists, sold to the Baptists, and soon found to be too small. Larger chapels were built in both Croyde and Georgeham and must have served an active, growing community. This situation is no doubt reflected in the Rector's rather bitter answer to the question in a questionnaire from the Bishop. "Have you any proposal to make?" Answer, "The only observation I presume to make is that the licensing of ignorant and uneducated Preachers has inundated the country with Sowers of sedition and heresy".

There was in fact considerable rivalry between church and chapel folk well over a hundred years later; one was either "church" or "chapel". In general, the landowners, their tenants and dependents were "church" and independent farmers and tradespeople were "chapel".

....

A bridge, as mentioned earlier, was built in Georgeham, across the stream below the church in 1868 by two locals, Richard Pearse and `Robert Scamp. There is still a stone in the wall next to Foote Farm bearing this information, although the date is difficult to decipher.

There was a suggestion in1828, by the Barnstaple Turnpike Trust, that a new road should be built joining Braunton, Georgeham, West Down, Mortehoe and Ilfracombe. Six objecting petitions were received from Georgeham. The road was never built.

....

In the 1830s it was decided that all remaining tithes paid in kind should be converted to cash, the value of each given officially. This resulted in a nation-wide survey. From it we have for Georgeham both the Tithe Map and the Tithe Apportionments which show exactly who owned and who tenanted what in 1839/40.

This shows that it remained normal to farm scattered fields, still reached by the old farm tracks. This was a result of holdings and tenancies being split by inheritance. One example is included here.

The map also shows some derelict properties. (There were to be 29 uninhabited houses by the 1891 census.). Two water mills existed in the parish, one below Forda the other at Croyde. There was a third mill at Heddon Mill. All were apparently still working into the 20th century.

The Tithe information states that 40% of the people owned less than half an acre; 13.8% had more than 50 acres. 81.4% of the land was arable, 10.6% was common land. However, those owning little land may well have been tenants of other lands.

Comparing an 1832 Land Tax list with the Tithe information it is clear that the 'manor' holdings had shrunk. The Harris holding in Pickwell, Georgeham and North Buckland had far more land in 1832 than is shown as belonging to its next owner, Lord Fortescue, by 1839.

As a result of the tithes enquiry it was decided that the rector would be paid £500 per annum, in cash, instead of some being paid in kind as previously.

It is increasingly difficult from this point to keep track of land holding as land was bought, sold, rented, and mortgaged both by locals and people from out-

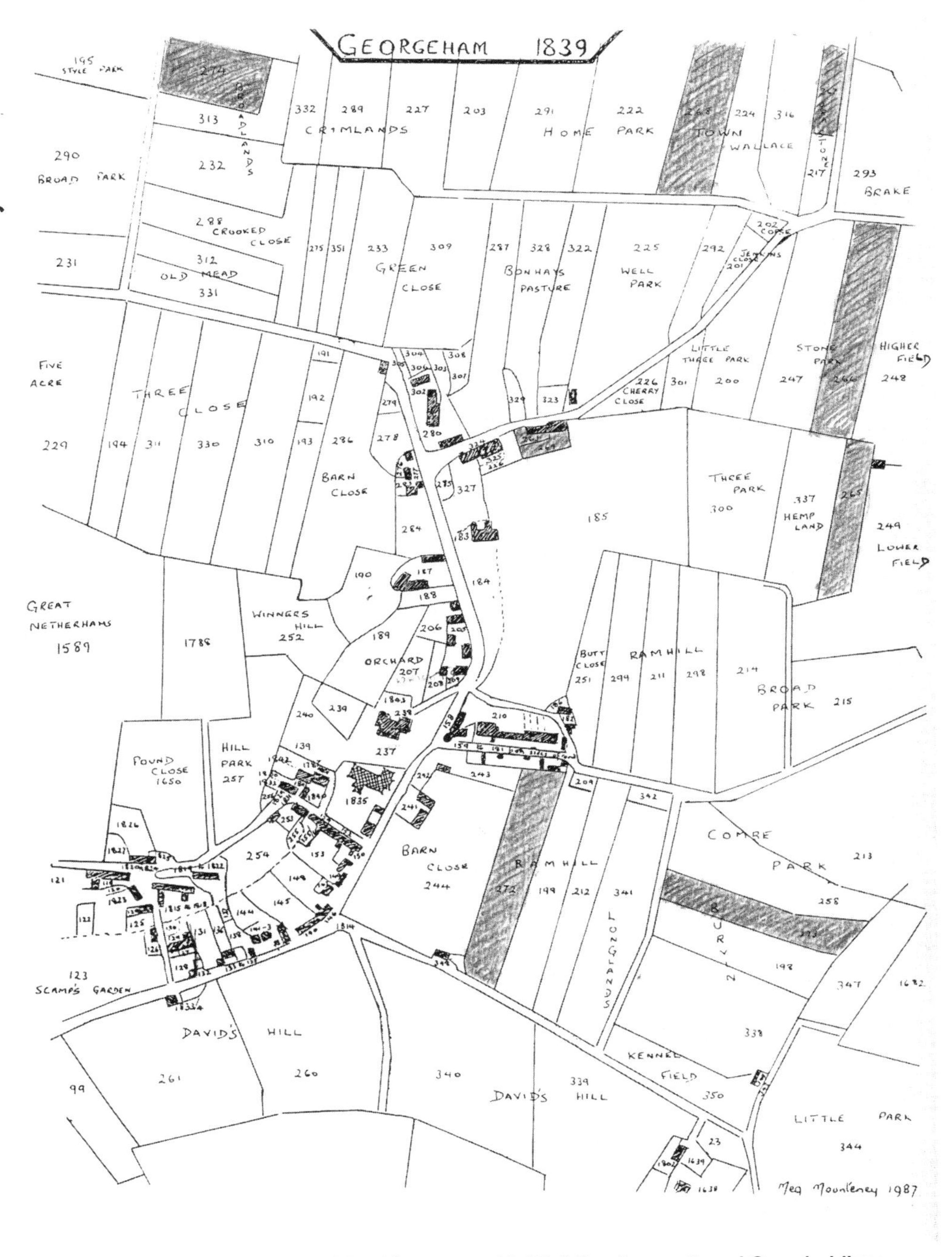

Georgeham Tithe Map, drawn by Meg Mounteney, highlighting the scattered Goss holdings.

side the area. By 1861 the Census mentions "paupers" for the first time.

....

Among the church papers is the Vestry Minute book for 1865 - 1893. Most entries are routine, but remind us that the parish was still the vehicle for local administration, dealing with the Poor Rate, road maintenance etc. More detail of the Vestry Book can be found in a later section, "The Vestry Book" In 1866 a notice was published asking if farmers would agree to a voluntary rate of 2d in the pound as an insurance against loss of cattle to plague. In 1871 two Constables were appointed, one for Georgeham, one for Croyde. Curiously,the unfortunate Constable for Georgeham, who in 1883 was stabbed and died in the course of what started as a drunken quarrel, is not listed as Constable in the Vestry Book.

William White's 1850 "Directory of Devon" says Georgeham had four blacksmiths, four pubs, many farmworkers, five boot and shoemakers. Other Directories tell of land owners, gentry, tradesmen, post and telegraph offices.

The manors of Georgeham, Pickwell and North Buckland were bought by Lord Fortescue in 1832/3, possibly in the hope that minerals might be found in useful quantities. There were mines, none too successful, at Spreacombe and North Buckland, and other sites were tried. The land was tenanted, but a survey was made for Lord Fortescue of his new estates. In Georgeham several people were found to have taken over bits of the manor property, including Mr Scamp who ran the Five Bells pub. Somebody else had built a pigsty on the manor waste. Rent was owing!

....

In fact, there was a general revival at the end of the century. The church was largely rebuilt in 1876, perhaps just as well as repairs were needed a few years before. The nave roof may have

The chancel at Georgeham Church before the quire stalls were removed in 2007

been lowered at this time, although it may have been done much earlier. The gallery was removed, the ornate ceiling disappeared too, the windows were gothicised, and pitch pine pews replaced the old oak box pews. Heavy handed perhaps, but thorough and the work revealed several ancient remains of an earlier building (See above) Much of this work was funded by the Rector, Francis Hole.

A new school was built in 1868, still in use today.

There was some mining activity in the area from 1861 at North Buckland and Spreacombe. This was never very successful and never made much impact among the local inhabitants. Further details are in the section "Mining"

At the end of the century a new phase began. Tourism. Trains began running to Ilfracombe in 1874, also ferries from South Wales. Braunton was our nearest station. Croyde had the earliest holiday homes and lodging houses.

....

Up until 1894 Parish administration was centred on the church. The church/vestry council levied and administered the Poor Tax and its Waywardens were responsible for the roads and public highways generally. The parish looked after its own patch, with two constables to uphold the law.

This council was very active. The Vestry Book gives us the names of village officials from 1864 to 1895. Obviously, the Rector was there, churchwardens who were mostly the larger landowners, but also many of the farming community had roles to play. As noted earlier, more detail can be found in "The Vestry Book" section. Braunton has a fuller collection of Vestry Books and churchwardens' accounts which record repairs to church and chapels, cutting trees, establishing parentage of children, providing clothing and taking a destitute lady back to her own parish (so that they could be responsible for her upkeep.)

In 1894 however the system changed and civil parishes were created. In the case of Georgeham the bounds remained much the same - and until recently these bounds were walked regularly. The new Parish Councils came under the District Councils and the County Councils. Centralisation had set in.

One suspects that this change was welcomed by some, resented by others.

The Parish Council Minutes

The first meeting of the new style Parish Council was on !st December 1894 and as can be seen from the accompanying reproduction of the Minutes the councillors were not very different from the list of officials taken from the Vestry Book. They met in the schoolroom. The Rev Hole was elected Chairman and subsequently signed each set of Minutes. Fortunately he only took the Minutes himself on rare occasions. His writing, other than his signature is not easy to decipher.

On 15th August 1895 there was a discussion about putting lamps at the most dangerous corners in the parish. It was also suggested that some form of Technical Education should be organised and courses and lectures given for young people during the winter.

At a later meeting they discussed sinking a well and providing a pump at Cross. It was suggested that they should accept the offer of part finance from the people in the cottages and supply the difference from Parish Council funds.

On 10th June 1896 it was proposed "that the new pump be boxed in, so as to prevent children from throwing stones and rubbish, and that a lock and key be provided." (A pump still stands in a recess in the wall between the cottages.)

In 1900 three Overseers were appointed; four in 1906.

In March 1905 Mr Style, owner of Pickwell Manor, was unanimously elected as school manager.

September 1905 saw a proposal that an application be made to the County Council for grants for lectures on Manures, Feeding Stuff and Sheep Shearing.

In 1907 it was reported that "the allotment gate only needed a few nails, which had been done"

Two entries show that there were problems changing from the previous system. The chairman and clerk had to look at the Vestry Book to find references "to percentage allowed owners of cottages let at, or less than £8 per year rent". Later, reference had to be made to the previous officials to see if they could change the investments of the charities (These charities were combined in 1910 into one fund for the relief of people in need).

One councillor complained of the inconvenience of having to take weights and measures to Braunton to be tested.

Subsequent entries show much discussion about wells and drains. There was much concern about drains, especially in Croyde, and about a choked drain at Darracott which was near a well.

In June 1908 it was judged that earth closets were best for dealing with the sewerage problem in Croyde!

In June 1910 the Parish Council decided to ask the District Council exactly where the wells were, and to ask that the Medical Officer should check the water.

At one meeting the parish proposed to borrow £200 for a new drainage system and that they should inform the District Council that they proposed to borrow the money.

In December 1910 the District Council was "respectfully asked to provide a supply of pure and adequate water to all ratepayers".

In 1911 however, the suggested system was so expensive "it would begger the parish" and they would write and ask why the parish's suitable springs were not being used.

The next meeting noted that various springs had been visited with the representative of the civil engineering firm and it had been recommended to supply water from the spring at Perrymans.

These are just a few examples, the complete Georgeham Parish Council Minutes are in Barnstaple Records Office.

Georgeham Parish Council.

December 31st 1894

We the undersigned do hereby declare that we undertake the Office of Parish Councillors for the Parish of Georgeham

W. V. Richards
George Downing
John Tucker
William Cranshey Dennis
John Webb
William Webb
Henry Wensley
Edwin Zeale
George Bale Smith.

It was proposed by Mr G. Downing and seconded by Mr W. V. Richards & supported by John Tucker & George Bale Smith that the Rev. W. Hole be elected Chairman.

Mr Zeale seconded by W. Webb & supported by J. Webb H. Wensley & W. C. Dennis moved as an amendment that Mr Dennis take the Chair

Carried 5 to 4.

Minutes of the first meeting of the Parish Council 1894, courtesy of NDRO and the Parish Council

8

This brings us almost up to date, with the 20th century. But the roads weren't made up with tarmac until the 1920s, some much later. The current road from Saunton to Croyde was built in 1906. Cattle were sold in the fields in 1908 to an agent and then collected up and driven to the market. Because the roads/tracks were narrow and banked only one person was needed. He took them and his horse about five miles when another man took over. The first man collected his horse and rode home. Fields were available at intervals to rest the cattle.

1906, the new road to Saunton, Mr Ted Morgan and visitors.

In a way the 1914 - 18 war made no great difference to village life. Although some of the men left to fight and some sadly did not return, and those who did, it was said, were never quite the same as before, life generally did not change dramatically. Much of the administration had been taken over by the Rural District Council and Devon County Council, but in many ways the village and parish remained very much in charge of their own affairs.

We have extracts from some of the Parish Magazines from this time which give us a good flavour of daily life.

Extracts from the Parish Magazine, 1907 - 1919

Major George Style, owner of Pickwell presented the parish with a drill hall and miniature rifle range. Eventually it became a house and is now Streamways Nurseries. And so we read in the magazine:

September 1907, that Georgeham and Croyde Rifle Range was formally opened by Major Style; that Mr Monk, of Forda, was also present and there was a concert and tea.

December 1908, after a jumble sale the month before which raised £1 15s 1d for the Parish Nurse Fund, the Nursing Committee presented Nurse Fox with a dressing bag and purse.

November 1909 there was a lecture, at the Rifle Range, on volcanoes and earthquakes, in aid of the District Nurse Fund. 10 tankards were presented, as prizes in a shooting competition.

In general, the Rifle Range served as meeting room, and dance/concert hall as well as a rifle range.

In June 1911 it was reported that George Lovering won a suit of clothes for shooting. Also that £61 7s 11d was collected for the Coronation, of which £50 was invested in the name of the parish.

The July 1912 magazine reveals that there had been a sheep shearing competition; champion was George Lovering. Meanwhile, members of the Night School had had an enjoyable evening.

In December 1910 a fund had been set up for the protection of bathers at Croyde, and in 1911 equipment was provided; a light cart filled with 2 cork life jackets, 2 floating throwing sticks each with 30 yards of line, 1 full size life buoy with ropes and floats, 1000 fathoms of light hawser on a reel. Two notice boards were placed, one at each end of the sands.

From notes taken from the original entries, it seems that the Poor Rate was still levied. In 1913 £364 8s 8d was collected. Payments were made to the District Council, Barnstaple Union, Highways and the Parish Council, which received £5

By October 1914 thirty-one young men from the parish were serving in the armed forces and in September the Rifle Range had been fitted with 8 beds.

January 1915 reports that Forda Convalescent Home was closed.
By May we had a Refugee Committee and a room was rented in Braunton for one refugee, a Mr Scholbert "where he can be found for veterinary work". Mr R Willon gave a flag pole and a large St George flag.

July 1916 notes "We possess a life saving apparatus on Croyde Bay Sands".

On a happier note, in December 1918 the magazine reports that there was a peel of bells on Armistice Day.

February 1919 notes that the new heating was finished in the church.
In June 1919 40 young demobbed men were entertained at the Rifle range by Mr and Mrs Monk.

In July two tablets were made, one for the church, one for the Baptist Chapel bearing the names of the six men who were killed in the war. It was decided that there should be a clock in the church tower as a War Memorial, funded by a house to house collection and by a 1d rate.

In October the same year Miss Hyde rented Mr Seldon's bungalow at Forda for the Parish Nurse and a stretcher was given to the parish, to be kept in Georgeham police station. (The policeman lived in a cottage on Netherham Hill.)

By November the church clock was available, at the price of £232, including fitting. But not including delivery. It was hoped that one of the farmers would bring it up from Braunton, with no charge.

After much argument it was voted in January 1920 that the clock face should be on the south face of the tower, perhaps adding one on the east face later.

Meanwhile, in December 1919 repairs were made to the 1500 gallon tank that held water to flush the school lavatories.

9

For the next 20 years we have various sources including the Parish Council Minutes and the Minutes for the new Village Institute - though for a more dramatic view of village life one should turn to Henry Williamsons book "The Village", or the twin volumes of his Life in and Tales of a Devon Village.Here you will find tales of daily life, local wildlife, squabbles about where the new cemetery should be built, extreme poverty, local landowners and much else vividly described. One should allow a little for artistic license!

The village was still peaceful, but by no means cut off. The first cars had appeared, although the roads did not have their modern surface. Visitors arrived to stay with relatives, travelling to Braunton station and then coming up over the hills in a horse and cart. They had to walk up the hills though!

In 1921 offertory bags were given to the church by Major Style of Pickwell Manor. Mr Stevenson-Balfour recorded that Major Style had turned the ivory rings, which held the bags open, from elephant ivory, and carved the handles from a black wood from Kenya. The bags themselves were made by Mrs Hudson who lived at Bye Cross House, and lined with the remains of long kid gloves.

The offertory bags were still in use in the 1970s . They were brought to the ends of the pews by the Sidesmen and passed along the pew, each person making their contribution.

....

We have a letter from the firm who tendered to take down the church bells and replace the beams that held them.

The church bells had needed maintenance at intervals since 1765. In 1894 Messrs Mears and Stainbank had done some work, and left their card in the bell tower, listing the weights and inscriptions of the bells. By 1926 major work was necessary.

Dated January 1926, this letter was sent from Messrs Mears and Stainbank of

Whitechapel Road, London. It says that they had examined the bells and that one had been recast in 1765. There was a peal of six bells, all cast in 1748 by Abel Rudell in Gloucester. "In key note they are a little short of F, concert pitch. They are in good tone and all appear perfectly sound" The bell frame however caused concern in that it was worm eaten in parts and too close to the walls so that it risked damage to the structure of the tower. The report seems very thorough and must have caused a good deal of worry. The estimated cost of the restoration was £294 10s.

In fact, Taylors of Loughborough won the contract to repair the bells and the frame. The bells went to the foundry. Most of the work on the frame was done on site , by local men under guidance from Taylors.

Two further bells were added at this time. One was given by Lady Robertson of Putsborough Manor.

The last bell was paid for by the parishioners who agreed on the inscription -
"My morning ring doth call them in"

Georgeham Parish Institute soon after its opening in 1926

This completed the peal of eight bells.

From 1926 we have extracts from the Parish Institute Committee. The Institute was set up as a social venue, replacing the Rifle Range. It was hoped to provide an alternative centre of activity to draw people away from the public houses! The Institute, now the Village Hall was built on the corner of Netherham Hill, opposite the Forge, on land given by Mr Lock and part financed by Col. Elliott of Pickwell.

Extracts from the Minutes of Georgeham Parish Institute.

January 19th, 1926 saw the first committee meeting. Two trustees are named, Miss Hyde from Croyde and Mr Lock. Several meetings in 1926 describe the setting up of the Institute. Mrs Hall was to be president of the Tea Committee, and the opening ceremony was to be a tea followed by a dance. Price of admission, tea and dance 1/6. People were asked to bring food for the table.

Miss Hyde asked if she could present three lamps. Mr Edwards, headmaster of the village school, would present one lamp. Sir Charles Hyde would present a piano. Mr Gammon, the caretaker, was provided with "1 bass broom, 1 dust pan and brush, 1 small mop, 7lb tin of soft soap, large hair brush for the floor, 2 buckets and a roll of dusters". 100 chairs were ordered.

By May the skittle alley was finished.

At the July meeting, attention was drawn to cases of rowdyism, bad behaviour and damage. Undaunted, it was decided in August to spend £10 on china, badged GPI (still in use until recently).

December 1926 brought a report of misconduct by younger members. By the end of the next year Col. Elliott had designed a weathercock incorporating St George and the Dragon also a sundial, to be attached to the dial on the south wall. The sundial is still there, but not the weathercock.

In October 1928 all the painting was finished. A notice was placed in the skittle alley forbidding the use of foul language.

A signboard and two manuscript pictures were being painted and were to be presented on Saturday, 12th January, at a social.

(The signboard has caused a certain amount of discussion. Pictures available show two different paintings - one of Etmar the Saxon, one of St George. It seems from the photos that there was a different painting on each side of the board. However, only the St George picture is remembered and a copy of that, painted by Miss Silvie, is in the Village Hall.)

Detail of the Parish Institute sign, showing the two different designs

In August the following year a letter of apology was received from Henry Williamson, who, with a friend had stuck newspaper over the sign. He had confessed and apologised to the rector who was chairman of the Institute Committee.

In December 1932 it was decided "that skittles must not be played while the hall is being used for a lecture, concert, whist drive, or other similar purpose".

The Institute had evidently become the centre of considerable social activity, because in August 1933 evenings were allotted for the following forthcoming events: 1) Social and dance; 2) Christmas Party; 3) Toy Symphony; 4) Minstrels; 5) Country dances; 6) Village band; 7) Concert; 8) Competitive Whist Drives or draughts by teams for prizes; 9) Quiet evening.

At another time there was to be a Hallowe'en party, or a lantern lecture.
In April 1938 Miss Kemp-Welch wrote offering to paint another sign, if somebody would take the old one down and prepare a new one.

In 1939, with a deteriorating international situation, Lieut. Squire asked if he could hire the Hall to drill the Georgeham section of the 6th Devon regiment. They hired it each Monday at a cost of 5/-.

On 14th August 1939 the hall was used for the distribution of gas masks, and in September it was closed "for the time being"

Apart from the Institute Minutes we know that there was a flood in 1931, recorded in the North Devon Journal Herald and also in Lois Lamplugh's book. After heavy rain there was a great surge of water down the stream which caused damage all down the valley. There was another less damaging flood in 1952.

DAILY HERALD JUNE 10TH 1931

AFTERMATH OF FLOODS

1931 flood at Georgeham (l). Newspaper cutting found at Braunton Museum
After the flood, outside Skirr Cottage (r).

....

Another author who lived in the village briefly was R V Thompson, describing the village in his "Home in Ham."

At some point the national time was adopted, so the sundial on the Village Hall is about 20 minutes slow! The village had an electricity supply in 1934 and also a sewer whose pipe ran down the cenre of the village, alongside the stream. There was, Mr Ben Isaac tells us, a huge septic tank in a field below the village which had to be emptied at intervals.

There was , however, no main water supply. Most farms and many houses had their own wells. For those who did not, there was a stream and rain water butts

Collecting drinking water from the pump outside The Haven

for washing and cleaning and public wells from which drinking water was fetched.

Families were still living in the tiny old cob cottages, damp, unless a fire burned continuously, but the worst of them had disappeared and 10 Council Houses had been built in Newbury Road.

Most of the remaining traditional manor property was sold off when Pickwell was sold in 1922. After that, other property came on to the market and a local builder, Porter Thomas, built several houses and bungalows including East Barn, Windsor Cottage, Stone Cottage, Wayside and Redcot.

More visitors were coming into the area. There was a bus link to Barnstable, via Braunton. Machinery appeared on the farms. There were also plans to continue the Marine Drive through from Woolacombe to Croyde, creating a coast road.

Land was sold above the beach at Vention, from the Pickwell Estate, for the development of several large houses. The Grey House was the home of Negley Farson an American author, and then his son Daniel. The Mitchell Hedges family had another.

Two hotels were built, one originally called Casa del Mare, becoming Putsborough Sands Hotel and then a block of flats above Putsborough beach. The other was built up on Heathercombe. In 1941 when it was in use as a school it caught fire and was destroyed, leaving only a forlorn chimney until the site was cleared sometime in the 1980s.

In the 1920s and 30s agriculture was not very profitable. Prices were low. At least one of the farmers' wives walked across to Woolacombe to try to sell her produce.

Still, there were compensations. Several farms had their own cider presses. One was at West End another at Putsborough.

The road to Higher Ham as it ran past Incledon House, 1930s

View of Putsborough Sands in the 1930s, showing the Putsborough Sands Hotel. In the distance is the hotel at Heathercombe. Also visible are some of the new houses being built above the beach.

10

Then came the 1939 - 1945 War. It stopped some changes; the Marine Drive was never continued. Local men served and were called up, although agriculture was an exempted occupation to some extent. Many of the farmers' wives and daughters worked on the farms more than ever. Evacuees arrived, families sometimes, or just children - some came back and settled later. Houses filled with relatives from London. At this time too, some of the fields were full of flowering bulbs in an attempt to keep a safe base for the bulb industry. The bus was, for a while, powered by a 'gas' unit which it towed along behind, smelling quite evil.

The beach sprouted huge posts (the bases still visible at some tides in 2007), lumps of concrete and rolls of barbed wire. Bombers from the air base at Chivenor used to swoop low over Baggy, over a concrete arrow which is still visible, to bomb a floating target in Putsborough Bay, and convoys of ships could be seen going up the Bristol Channel, sometimes with attendant aircraft.

The beach at Vention showing the huge posts placed all along the beach as defences during the war (1946), and the remains of one post in 2007. Remains of one of the huge posts driven into Putsborough beach during the war. Still visible at some tides (r) (VAM)

A Home Guard company was formed - No. 27 Platoon "A" Company, 25th Ilfracombe Battalion, in 1944. Many families still have a photograph of the company, taken outside the Parish Institute. The men met for drill and training. There were various installations locally including some sandbagged earthworks near Black Rock. There is a list of the men in the "Inhabitants" section.

And yet, the cows came in for milking through the village, the sheep were driven along the lanes; sand blew over the road in Croyde and Saunton; corn was harvested; the blacksmith continued to mend machinery, and cartwheels and shoe horses and Miss Hudson sold the most wonderfully sticky lemon and honey sweets from her little house on the Putsborough road.

There was great excitement when late in the war the Americans came into the area to train for the D-Day landings.

11

More Minutes of the Georgeham Parish Institute

The Institute Minutes continue again when it reopened in 1944. Mr Lock resigned his Trusteeship due to deafness. The first Minute Book was to be placed, with the deeds in Lloyds Bank in Barnstaple so that a record of his gift could be preserved. Deeds of the Institute in Col. Elliott's name were to be recovered and placed in the same bank in the name of the rector of Georgeham.

On 3rd May 1945 the Parish Council asked to use the hall for VE Day, which was imminent.

In February 1946 a 'Welcome Home' dance was to be arranged and the Welcome Home Fund would be distributed. Sadly seven men had been killed. (A Memorial Screen bearing their names was later placed in the church, separating the space at the bottom of the tower from the nave).

Finally in 1949 a letter stated that the skittle cup was lodged with Lloyds bank in Barnstaple.

Later Minutes are now stored in Barnstaple at the North Devon Records Office. The Parish Institute became the Parish Hall, but activities there continued with dances, film shows, a youth club and of course, skittles.

....

The local branch of the Women's Institute was formed in the village in 1948 and has, as well as fulfilling the usual national functions, been an excellent social and organising hub ever since.

After the war, tourism took off. Cars became common, along with car parks near the beaches.

In the 1950s many of the farms that had until then been tenanted were bought by the tenants and for the next 30 years agriculture became relatively profitable.

In this area however mixed farming remained the norm. Milk came straight from the farm to the doorstep well into the 1960s, and although combine harvesters in the narrow lanes were dreaded by visitors, some things remained traditional. On a small patch of land, now part of Davids Hill, one farmer was to be seen broadcasting seed from an Ostermilk can with a paddle beneath swinging on a piece of string round his neck!

The second flood in 1952 was less destructive than the earlier one but knocked down garden walls and flooded the low lying properties. In 1952 mains water was brought to the village and the public well in Netherham Hill was sealed.

The Village Hall hosted a youth club in the 1950s and Saturday nights saw a village dance attended by a good range of ages.

People began moving into the area when they retired, buying some of the old houses.

The Horticultural Society used to meet at the Village Hall and Gordon Norman has kindly provided a picture of the club in the late 1940s or early 1950s, showing, amongst others - Mr Hopkins, holding the cup; Nurse Jeffries; Mrs Sharples, Jennifer and Stephen; Mr Lawrence, the Baptist minister; Mrs Pester; Mary Hancock; Mrs Kelland; Mrs Jones; Mr Bartlett; Rupert Colwell; Bill Tanner; Mr Thody, and (sitting) Jeremy Thody; Mr Pugsley; Mrs Gammon; Mrs Turner; Donald Reeves and Fred Crow, coastguards; Mrs Crow.

Croyde opened its own Village Hall in 1952. Cecil Parsons' film of its opening survives.

Georgeham School still served both villages and the rest of the parish, but over the next thirty years the school numbers fluctuated and declined. Fewer people lived and worked in the village. Fewer people worked on the farms. Often the younger generation moved out to find work, to Braunton, Barnstaple or anywhere work and affordable housing were available.

More and more visitors however came to the beaches, traffic jams became common in the summer, especially with the coaches which ran tours from Ilfracombe. Many houses offered Bed and Breakfast accommodation and most farms had camping and caravan sites.

With the tension of the Cold War in the early 1960s the old village wells were again investigated and their condition listed, as had been done at the start of the war in 1939.

Two more books were written by a resident author. For a few years from 1970 a little donkey trap could be met in the lanes, and its driver, Daisy Baker, wrote two charming books about her experiences exploring the lanes from her base in Spreacombe.

12

In the 1980s and 1990s house prices continued to rise. Most of the old cottages were modernised,; sometimes two small cottages were converted to one larger cottage. Eventually 28% of the houses became second homes.

At this stage it was proposed to build an estate on Davids Hill. The original plan would have completely swamped the old village, with 100 homes built on 7.7 acres. This was toned down, and eventually 48 homes were built; small bungalows for older couples and larger homes for families.

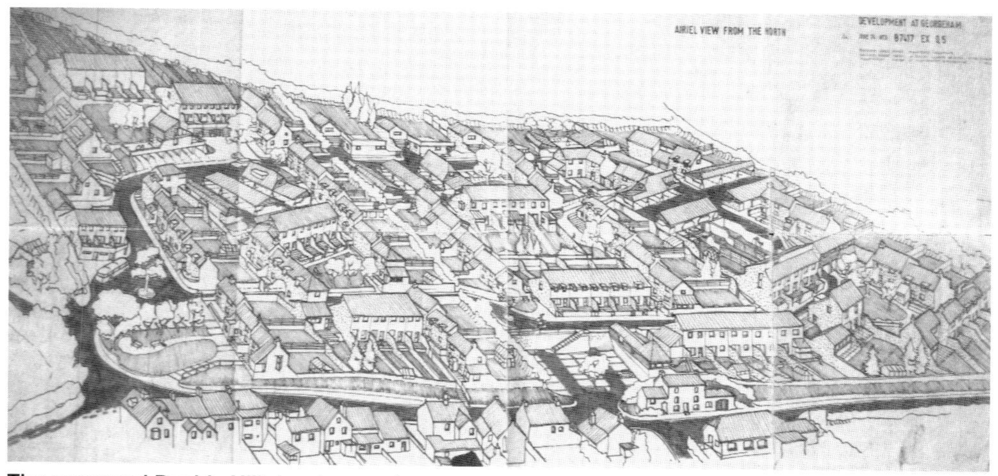

The proposed Davids Hill development.

Meanwhile community life in Georgeham continued to flourish. In 1958 the Parish Institute became the Village Hall. Eventually, the hall was found to be too small and a small extension, the result of much fundraising, was ceremonially opened in 1985.

The Parish Church and the Baptist Chapel were centres of activity. The Bellringers had taken up their (purely voluntary) duty again after the war. There were two grocers' shops for a while, one also selling meat. The Post Office moved down opposite the lych gate and stayed there until it was incorporated into the one remaining, and current, village shop.

In 1956 it was felt that young people in the village needed somewhere to play. With money left over from the War Memorial fund (only half had been used to provide the screen in the church) and with money raised and borrowed by the eight Trustees, the current Playing Field was bought. Swings and a roundabout were provided for the children, and a football pitch for the older boys, leaving lots of room for everyone to run about as they liked.

This field was the venue for many years for village fetes and Guy Fawkes Night bonfires, all organised by energetic villagers along with the original Trustees. The Silver Jubilee in 1977 saw a particularly lively fete here with all kinds of events including wheelbarrow races. A film of this still exists. In 1993 ownership of the field was passed to the Parish Council which became its trustees.

The Women's Institute celebrated the Millennium by creating a garden near the bus stop, which had moved into its current stone buildings when Davids Hill was developed.

Increasingly people worked in Barnstaple and beyond, and then, when surfing became really popular, younger people began to move in - or back. Computers mean that people can live and work here, going to London or wherever as necessary.

There is a huge tourist influx in the summer and an increase in visitors generally, all year round, creating more work locally, giving employment to a growing number of small businesses and services.

The downside of all this activity is that young locals are priced out of the housing market. There are no cheap houses in the village. Some are second homes, empty for most of the year. Others are let to holiday makers at high weekly rents.. Only the smallest houses sell for less than £300,000, and rents are commensurate and short tenure. We were lucky, when the Glebe was developed to secure ten social housing units including three small bungalows. The development, though much opposed, also provided a much-needed car park and an open area, which it is hoped will develop into a village green.

In 2008 it is good to review what we have lost, what remains and what has developed. We have records of our early history, most of which can be consulted at the local Records Office in Barnstaple. The church tower dominates the village and the church is very much a presence here. For all of us New Year is rung in by the ringers. The plough is blessed in January,. Easter is celebrated. The Harvest Festival service is followed by a Harvest Supper in the Village Hall, food brought and shared, in the tradition of the old Parish Institute; and of course there are the Christmas services. Appropriate flags are flown from the mast on the church tower; the Church flag, the simple cross of St. George and the Union Jack. The church too sees our Baptisms, Weddings and Funerals.

Lost currently is the Ham Revel, a robust celebration following St George's Day - possibly just as well. Lent Shirt Night, when the lads used to play practical jokes, still fondly remembered in conversations between Mr Balfour and some older members of the village, is now forgotten.

The church choir which led singing in the 40s, 50s and 60s, (ladies wearing white headdresses, otherwise normal clothes, and later all members wearing deep blue robes), no longer exists, and the Baptist Chapel has closed for services.

The village school, the old one with new additions is thriving. Children still perform the Broom Dance at fetes, but the tradition of them dancing round the Maypole at various points in the village has gone.

Georgeham Village Fete, 2006

The Village Fete however, held on the playing field has been revived. Currently it is energetically organised by CASC (the joint committee of the local sports clubs), the aim being to raise funds to upgrade the playing field with new facilities for sport, a new children's play area and most expensive of all, a pavilion where players can change, a meeting room, and a covered terrace from which games can be watched and children supervised.

....

So the village has slowly changed. Its administration, as far as we know, began in Saxon times with the township and the hundred. In Norman times the manor-based administration overlaid this, but did not replace it. The church became more of a focus for administration after Henry VIII made church based-parishes responsible for much of it, including roads. This system survived actively until 1894 when civil parishes were introduced, linked to the District and County Councils. We still have the Parish Council, but its duties and powers are minimal compared with those of the church based parishes of 1538 - 1894.

This is a brief history of the village, much detail has been omitted, and for that, and if any offence has been committed by leaving out important local events, I apologise.

Inhabitants

In no way can I emulate Henry Williamson and write vividly of the inhabitants of Georgeham and the surrounding area. And I wouldn't dare!

However, over the centuries until recently most of the people were involved in farming one way or another. There were the main landholders whose chief interest, no doubt, was in how much the land would yield in terms of income; there were tenant farmers who probably formed the solid backbone of the area and whose prosperity or otherwise depended on their farming of the land; there were farm workers who owned a bit of land but who also worked for the larger farms; there were also workers who moved round from farm to farm as itinerant labourers and other locals who specialised in rabbit trapping and the like. No doubt too, there were people who, particularly when times were difficult for agriculture, were unable to provide for their families and needed help from the parish to survive. Buyers and sellers of produce, tradesmen of all sorts, a few professional people - solicitors, doctors, schoolteachers and of course the rector, are all recorded. At intervals, from the nineteenth century retired sea captains and army officers occupied some of the larger houses.

We have several "snap shots" of the inhabitants. The spelling of their names is very variable. The earlier ones are interesting because they show a continuation of local names; the later ones, from the various Directories, because they show the range of people here - though they don't show rabbit trappers, itinerant workers or even ordinary working people.

Females only ever occur in these lists if they were property holders in their own right.

....

The earliest list is the Devonshire Lay Subsidy of 1332, which was a tax paid by all, on movable goods. The church was exempt and presumably there were people who had nothing taxable.

Pickwell, including Georgeham:

Robert de Cruwes	12d	Isobel de Sancto Albino	12d
Henry de Merwood	12d	Jordan de Vautort	12d
Andrew atte Hole	8d	John de Luscote	12d
John Horn	8d	John le King	8d
Philip Forster	8d	Richard Hoyte	8d
Richurde	8d	Thomas Hors	8d
Walter Dawe	8d	Arnulph Coppe	8d

(Richard de Pidkwill was taxed in South Molton, 8d)

Buckland Dynham (North Buckland)

Richard de Chambernoun	3-0d	Geofrey Yolde	20d
John Bonde	2-0d	John Jordyng	18d
Robert Konibere Knyght	2-4d	John Knyght	20d
Nicholas Pours	2-2d	William Shote	20d

Cridho (Croyde)

Baldwin Flemyng	5-0d	William Seuere	12d
Thomas Botoun	15d	William Loof	9d
William Taillour	16d	Mauger atte Ford	16d
Walter Gautel	10d	William Gauntel	8d
Robert Chaillou	12d	Philip Gadel	12d
William Coppe	10d	Walter Bysshop	18d
Hugh Rauf	15d	Walter atte Ford	9d
Henry Lytle	8d	Walter Lof	2-4d
Richard Copyner	14d	William Frere	20d
Thomas Gryffyn	12d	Edward Moryn	16d
William Maymond	8d	Stephen Bakere	18d
Thomas Gryffyn	8d	Robert Henry	8d
Robert Taillour	10d	Reginald Allysaundre	12d
Walter Alysaundre	12d	Arnulf Fot	9d
Joan Jacob	9d	Walter Broun	10d

....

Another fascinating list is from the Muster Roll of 1559. At this stage as in Saxon times, the parish was required to provide arms and men. This list was drawn up when Elizabethan England was preparing for a possible Spanish attack. Richer men were required "by statute" each to provide specified arms.

For example, John Newcourt (Pickwell) had to provide 3 corslets, 1 pike, 1 harquebus, 1 morion, 1 sheaf (24) of arrows and 1 steel cap. The parish had to provide 2 corselets, 2 pikes, 2 calivers (muskets), 2 murrions (sort of helmet). Among the archers were listed Thomas and George Bowhaye, William Incledon, and Henry Courtney.

Among the pikemen were Thomas Scampe, James Crascombe, Thomas Peryn. Billmen included Philip Tallin, John Tooker, Thomas Crascombe and Richard Hartnoll.

....

The Protestation Return for the parish in 1641, a hundred years later, includes among the 200 or so names Baglole, Barne, Bishoppe, Booden, Cloutman, Coney, Courtney, Croscombe, Gamon, Geenes, Hancock, Hartnoll, Harris, Heddon, Heywarde, Horwood, Knill, Little, May, Newcourt, Pearde, Perreman, Rashley, Richards, Scampe, Sweete, Thorne, Tooker, Upcott, Webber, Wheddon, and John Berrye, (Rector).

Just 21 years later in 1662, forty-seven people were listed to pay the Hearth Tax. Most of them had only one or two hearths, but William Newcourt (Pickwell) had 9, as did the Rector, Mr Thomas Colley.

Among the names on the list we have Sweet, Bourden, Tallin, Bagster, Richards, Croscombe, Hartnole, Tucker, Tooker, Harris, Rashlie, Scampe, Conny and Walter.

....

The next list I have is the Land Tax Assessment, 1732, "granting an aid to His Majesty George II", levied at 2 shillings in the pound. It includes John Harris (Pickwell), Rev. William Chichester (Rector), Samuel Sweet, George Wright, Hugh Isaac, Robert Incledon, Esq., Mary Deans, Peter Crascombe, Elizabeth Perryman, Mary Berry, John Ackland, Richard Talling, Thomas Hartnoll, Peter Parminter, Elizabeth Phare, William Moule, John Peard, Edward Chugg, Richard Heddon, Christopher Irwin, Richard Tucker, Paul Bagster.

....

There is also a list of parishioners in 1791, another Land Tax Assessment.

Mr Balfour found the list of "The Company of Georgeham Volunteers, April-May 1799.

Lieut. Prole, Captain.
Serg. Jasper Thomas
Serg. John Challacombe
Corp. James Britter
Corp. James Mock
Drummer James Howard

2nd Lieut. John Peard
Serg. Peter Goule
Serg. Thomas Lethebay
Corp. William Slocomb
Drummer John Thurlow

Among the 65 listed Privates were:
Paul Bagster, John Bennet, Philip Bishop, John Brimley, John Butler, John Cann, John Clibbett, James Conebear John Deane, Richard Gammon, John Hancock, John harding, James Hartnoll, Robert Horwood, Richard Joanes (sic), George Lewis, John Lock, John Lovering, George Norman, John Phillips, Phillip Richards, Robert Scamp, George Shapland, William Thomas, Richard Tucker, David Williams,

These men, and others had volunteered to defend the area against a possible French invasion.

....

Our next list comes from the Vestry Book, 1864 - 1894. This shows the elected officers of the parish at the time. The lists are in the section *The Vestry Book*.

....

Finally, we have the list and the photo too, of the Home Guard, formed by volunteers in the Second World War.

Back row (l-r): C Turner, C Brown, W Brown, F Irwin, J Isaac, T Beer, S Baggett, E Shapland, S Woolacott, H Edes, P Baggett, A Brown, F Bowden

Middle row (l-r): K Sarsfield, R Hancock, R Tucker, W Woolacott, J Taylor, P Elliot, F Gammon, T Phisick, G Tucker, L Kelland, S Elliot, A Hancock, Willis

Seated (l-r): A Smith, A B Thomas, Corp. J Pile, Serg. D Jones, Serg. J Gammon, Mitchell Hedges, Serg. Antell, Serg. Bartlett, Corp. Ben Isaac, Corp. R Gammon, W Lock, W Bawden

The Home Guard, WWII

Directories

The following information is taken from the Post Office Directory of Devonshire for 1866. (HSB's notes)

Earl Fortescue is Lord of the Manor.
Chief landowners: Mr Dunning, W V Richards Esq., Rev. F Hole.
Population in 1861: 873.
Parish Clerk: Robert Webber.
Schoolmaster: John Bale.
The Rev. Francis Hole, MA, JP, The Rectory.
William Vellacott Richards, Esq., Incledon House.
Western, Esq.

Commercial: Georgeham.
George Baggott, farmer.
John Bennett, shopkeeper
George Downing, farmer
Gabriel Bale, farmer
George Butler, shoemaker
William Gammon, blacksmith

Thomas Geen, shoemaker
William Geen, shoemaker
Joseph Goss, Rock House
Philip Goss, tailor
John Hunt, shopkeeper
Wm. Lang, tailor and beer retlr.
Geo. Menhinnett, tailor
John Mock, mason
Richard Pearse, mason
David Lock Roach, farmer
James Sanders, blacksmith
Robert Scampe, Ring of Bells and maltster

Charles Thomas, carpenter and Kings Arms
Richard Tucker, farmer
Robert Webber, farmer
Richard Zeale, shopkeeper.

North Buckland.
John Barnes, farmer
George Boyles, farmer
Richard Howard, farmer
George Smith, farmer
John Tucker, farmer
Richard Tucker, farmer
Thomas Tucker, farmer.

Darracott.
William Hancock, farmer
Thomas Harding, farmer

Putsborough.
Capt. Stanley Alvin
*George Downing, farmer
James Quick, farmer
George Ticker, farmer

Croyde of course is also listed.

* This may be an error. George Downing is also listed earlier, and actually farmed at Pickwell.

The Vestry Book

In his 1965 book, Mr Balfour wrote of a Vestry Minute Book which was in the church safe. It is now in the Records Office in Barnstaple. There was only one Vestry Minute Book, the one for 1865 - 1893. In some parishes more Vestry Books have survived. Sometimes there are also Churchwardens' Accounts for about 200 years. These are the records from when the church parish was responsible for much of what happened in the parish - looking after the poor, or sending them back to their parish of origin, repairing roads, collecting taxes, allocating them etc.

The Parish Officers - wardens, churchwardens, Assessors of Taxes, Overseers of the Poor - were elected by "the ratepayers of this parish" called to a meeting in the Vestry room.

Most of the entries in the Minute Book are, Mr Balfour said, quite mundane, but some he copied as being of interest.

On 11th March, 1865 a meeting wanted to make a rate for the repairs to the church; it was fixed at 1d in the pound, according to the Poor Rate value.

On 15th April 1865 it was proposed that a petition be drawn up against the redistribution of the Poor Rate in Unions.

On 3rd February 1866 a meeting was called to appoint a Cattle Inspector.

On 24th a a notice went up to see if farmers would agree to a voluntary rate of 2d in the pound as an insurance against the loss of cattle by plague.

On 25th April 1867 a ¼d rate was levied for the church to provide things necessary and proper for the due and decent celebration of Divine Service.

In 1870 Mr Roach was appointed Overseer by a majority of 8 votes. His work was specified -

To make all Poor Rates and collect all monies on the same; to attend all Vestry meetings and do all writing required; attend before the auditors to have all his accounts audited; to do all the work incidental to the office of Overseer and to travel from the parish for any purpose in the execution of his office. His pay was £12 per year.

In 1871 the ratepayers assembled in the Vestry thought it unnecessary to appoint constables, but at the next meeting they complied with the requirement from the magistrates and appointed two constables.

In 1872 they considered whether they should pay John Fowler £4 above his contract for repairing the road to Saunders Farm.

In 1873 a committee was formed to inspect a field called Freshwell (Croyde) in the occupation of Capt. Heddon with the idea of widening the road to the extent of 16 feet and building a wall. (There were often problems about whether a road was private or public and thus who was responsible for its upkeep)

Assessing property for the Poor Rate was one of their jobs. The rate for Mr Hole's plantation was raised from £1 17s 6d to £2 15s 11d. Earl Fortescue's wood's value was raised from £5 7s 6d to £6 12s 6d. Buckland and Spreacombe mines were also rated.

Mr Balfour also copied the lists of Churchwardens, Assessors of Taxes, Assistant Overseers and Waywardens from 1864 - 1895, taken from the Vestry Minute Book. They are reproduced here. Reference to the Directories will show where these people lived in the parish.

Lists of officials from the Vestry Book, 1864 - 1895

There were two Churchwardens each year, one for the Minister, one for the parishioners.

From **April 1864 - May 1867**, they were W V Richards (Incledon House) and W Lang.
May 1867 - April 1871 they were Capt. Alven (Putsborough Manor) and R Webber. (North Hole)
April 1871 - April 1874 they were John Tucker and R Webber

April 1874 - April 1889 they were Joshua Downing (Pickwell) and R Webber
April 1889 - April 1891 they were George Downing and R Webber
April 1891 - April 1895 they were George Downing (Pickwell) and John Tucker

The Assessors of taxes		The Overseers
1864/65	D L Roach	J Tucker, G Bagster
1865/66	D L Roach, G Smith, sen.	C Forest, R Tucker, W Hancock, W Quick
1866/67	D L Roach, R Webber	W Quick, W Howard, W Hancock, H Moule G Webber, J Barnes
1867/68	D L Roach, R Webber	W Hancock, H Moule, G Webber, J Barnes, A Western, G Smith
1868/69	D L Roach, R Webber	G Webber, J Barnes, A Western, G Smith, R Connibear, J Tucker sen.
1869/70	D L Roach, R Webber	A Western, G Smith, R Connibear, J Tucker sen. (Croyde,) G Downing, J Roach.
1870/71	R Webber, J Roach	R Connibear, G Downing, J Roach, J Lee, G Jones, W Harding.
1871/72	R Webber, J Roach	J Lee, G Jones, W Harding, W V Richards, W Smith sen., J Tucker, (Castlestreet)
1872/73	R Webber, J Roach	W Harding, W Hancock, W Smith, jnr., J Tucker (Castlestreet), R Jones, T Tucker.
1873/74	R Webber, J Roach	W Smith, J Roach, J Tucker (Castlestreet), R Jones, T Tucker, J Tamlyn.
1874/75	J Lee, J Roach	R Jones, T Tucker, J Downing, J Tamlyn, G Bagster, R Webber.
1875/76	W Quick, J Roach.	J Tamlyn, G Bagster, E Packer, G Bament
1876/77	W Quick, G Menhinnit	J Tamlyn, G Bament, C H Child, W V Richards, G Bagster, G Tucker E Packer.
1877/78	W Quick, G Menhinnit	W V Richards, G Bament, J Barnes, jnr., C H Child, R G Prole (Putsborough Manort), J Harding.
1878/79	R G Prole, E Zeale	J Barnes jnr., C H Child, R G Prole, T Harding, G B Smith, H Gammon
1879/80	R G Prole, E Zeale	C H Child, J Harding, G B Smith, H Gammon, J Tucker jnr., H Webber
1880/81	H Western, E Zeale	G B Smith, H Gammon, J Tucker jnr

	(Castlestreet), H Webber, W Harding, W Hancock.
1881/82 as above	J Tucker jnr. (Castlestreet), H Webber, W Harding, W Hancock, J Quance, J White.
1882/83 as above	W Harding, W Hancock, J Quance, J White, R Jones, C Tucker.
1883/84 as above	J Quance, J White, C Tucker, J Mock, T Tucker, W Tucker.
1884/85 as above	C Tucker, J Mock, T Tucker, W Tucker, R Prole, G B Smith.
1885/86 as above	T Tucker, W Tucker R G Prole, W Reed, T Gammon, G B Smith
1886/87 E Zeale, D L Roach	R G Prole, G B Smith, W Reed, T Gammon, Capt. Gammon, H Winsley.
1887/88 D L Roach, G B Smith	W Reed, T Gammon, Capt. Gammon, H Winsley, Capt. T Heddon, A Stoneham, W V Richards.
1888/89 as above	A Stoneham, W V Richards, T Heddon, H Windsley, W Lerwell, W Dyer, W Quick.
1889/90 as above	H Windsley, W Lerwell, W Dyer, W Quick, G Webber, W Gammon.
1890/91 D L Roach*, J Tucker	W Dyer, W Quick, G Webber, W Gammon, J Perriman, J Bagster.
1891/92 as above	J Perriman, G Bagster, G Smith, E Zeale, W Hancock, W Smith.
1892/93 as above	E Zeale, G Smith, W Hancock, G Bament, H Gammon.
1893/94 E Zeale, G Webber	J Crang, T Lang, W Hancock, G Bament. W Smith, H Gammon.

*D L Roach died 1892/3

A quick cross referencing of some of these names is interesting:

George Bagster was a farmer in Croyde
David Lock Roach farmed in Georgeham

W Quick, Home Farm, Croyde
W Harding farmed at Darracott
W Hancock farmed at Darracott
C H Child, farmer and cornmiller. Fig Tree
G Bament, farmed at South Hole
George Bale Smith was a farmer
J Quance farmed North Hole
W Reed farmed Ruda and had apartments
Edwin Zeale farmed in Croyde
W Lerwell farmed at North Buckland
George Menhennit was a tailor from Croyde.

There is also a list of Waywardens and Assistant Overseers. The same names occur, with the addition of J and Jas. Buckingham.

W Gammon and W Brooks were appointed Constables 1871 - 1873.

In 1889 R Webber was appointed Guardian of the Poor.

There were two W V Richards, father and son, both lived at Incledon.
The third generation became a bank manager in Barnstaple.

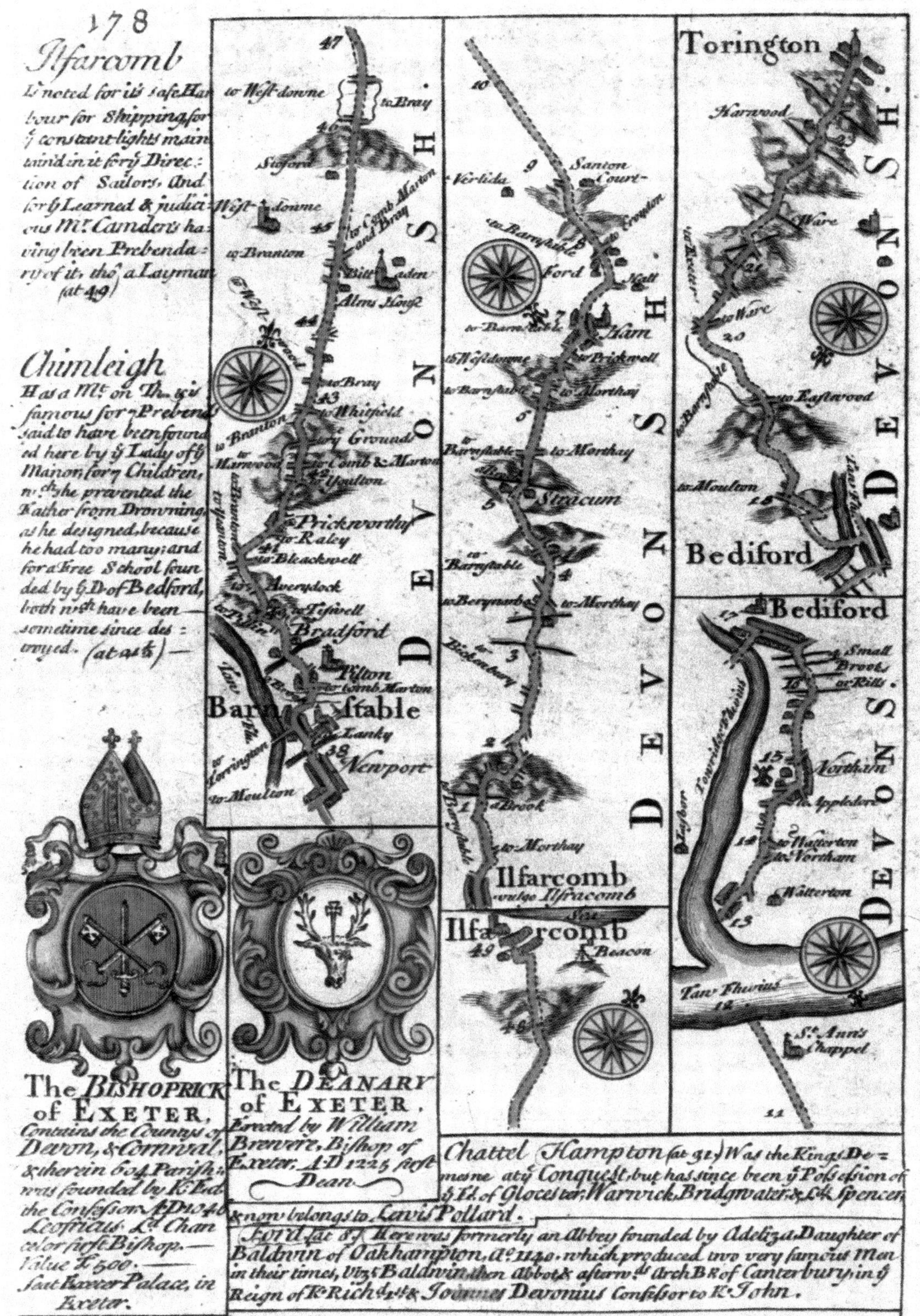

Ogilby's Map 1675

Spirit of Georgeham, Brian Pollard

Georgeham 1947

Sundial, Georgeham Church (SM)

Georgeham Church (SM)

In the snow, taken from the car park, 2009 (VAM)

A decorative panel in the Village Hall, c 1926, showing some of the common village names

Vention, the old limeburners cottages. Pre 1945

Putsborough Beach, the closest beach to Georgeham village, 2003 (VAM)

Georgeham, 2001

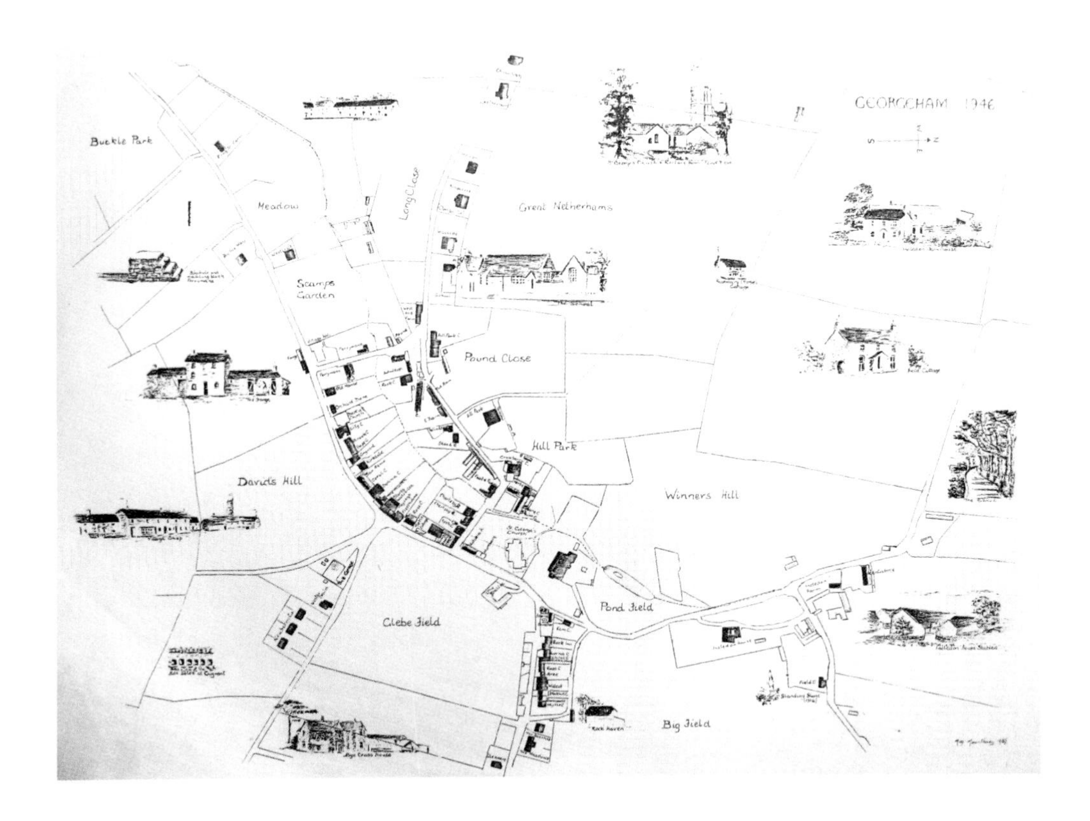

This elegant map shows and names most of the houses in Georgeham in 1946. It was drawn by Meg Mounteney in 1987 and she added sketches of some of the buildings in the style of the line drawing postcards which were sold in the 1940s and 1950s

The Baptist Chapel,
Georgeham (SM)

Landholding

To uncover the way land has been held in the area is an extremely difficult task. I have gathered some information. Hopefully, more of the puzzle will be revealed in the future.

Going right back to when the British tribes who lived in the south west and whom the Romans called Dumnonii and who were later called the West Welsh, we have little information. Their language was similar to that used in Wales at the time - presumably their social organisation was similar too, with minor local "kings" and a possible overall leader if there were anyone capable of imposing his authority over a variable area.

It is unlikely that there was much, if any, Roman influence, although legend suggests that the south west was part of the civilised Romano-British culture which struggled to survive the threat of the Saxons. Wales and Cornwall were involved. A recent Time Team dig revealed a trading post at Padstow importing wares from all over the Mediterranean world, and it is quite likely that North Devon was also. Perhaps to a lesser extent. However, the age of local "kings" continued throughout the Roman era and subsequently. One sad result of this trade was that the inhabitants were vulnerable to the plague which caused havoc in the 5th century.

The Christianising of the area by Welsh and Irish missionaries would not have affected landholding, though it might (according to the legend of St. Brannock) have changed their methods of cultivation. If the locals, in the 6th century needed to be introduced to ploughing it suggests a very isolated community. Gildas tells of disasters and plague among the people, and of course rumours of a Saxon advance had caused some migration to Brittany.

Fortunately the Saxon kingdoms fought among themselves and were at least officially Christian by the time that the West Saxon king, Ine, killed the last Prince of Dumnonia, Geraint, in 710.

By 857 the area was well and truly Saxon. We have the first actual reference when King Ethelbold gave 10 hides (about 1200 acres) of his royal manor of

Braunton to Glastonbury Abbey. At this point the small settlement of Ham may also have existed, just a few farming families owing allegiance to one of the Saxon nobles.

Peaceful development was interrupted all over the country at this point by Viking raids and armies, until Alfred (871 - 899) was able to re-establish Wessex.

King Edgar (957 - 975) regained the manor of Braunton by swapping it for some land in Somerset. Edgar was a great builder of churches and a great organiser. One of his close aides was Ordgar - who held Croyde, and whose daughter became the king's wife.

This sounds very civilised and modern, but only 30 years earlier, of King Athelstane it was said "In this year King Athelstane, Lord of Warriors, Ring-giver of Men, with his brother the prince Edmund, won deathless glory with the edge of swords in warfare... With their hammered blades the sons of Edward clove the shield wall and hacked the linden bucklers as was instinctive in them, from their ancestry, to defend their land, their treasure, and their homes, in frequent battle against the enemy." Quoted in 'The Normans and Their World' by Jack Lindsay.

From the time of King Edgar, and indeed before, landholding was simple. It all belonged to the king. Some he kept, the rest was granted out to the most important people and the church. In the case of the former, the grant carried with it duties, mostly military. The land grants were huge. Ordgar, already mentioned, was said to hold land in every village from Exeter to Frome - and, as we know, more in the south west. He was a 'minister' and 'ealdorman', an adviser to the king - an administrator in fact, nationally. His holdings therefore were looked after by others who in turn had obligations to him, and were farmed by a selection of freemen and slaves, some probably remnants of the original British inhabitants.

Some smaller parcels of land were granted directly by the king to less important individuals, often thanes, in return for a specific duty. This was done by charter, or book, and in Devon these lands often kept the name of Bookland or Buckland (Finberg).

Since the land belonged to the king it could be, and often was, granted in exchange for support, money, favours, and so changed overlords on a whim. The farming community (from free tenants to slaves) stayed put and provided some continuity, and a continuous supply of food and materials, weather permitting.

The country, at least in the south, was organised into shires, hundreds and townships. This was the channel for civil administration. People from each township had to go and meet at the centre of their Hundred. This organisation continued through Canute's Danish rule. He took Wessex under his personal control, but didn't alter civil administration to any extent. The system was still working in 1086 when the information for the Domesday Book was collected, and indeed into the 14th century.

From Reichel's "Hundreds of Braunton and Shirwell", quoting Feudal Aids, we learn that on 20th February 1316, the Parliament of Lincoln required each township to provide one man at arms.

The townships are listed and the names of the townships and of the Hundreds are given.

The lord of the Hundred of Braunton was the Abbott of Cleve, and the lord of Shirwell Hundred was John de Beaumont.

Croyde was in a township with Saunton, South Lobb (Lobb Philip), and Bradwell Pyne and associated hamlets. Baldwin Flemming was lord of the township, which was in Braunton Hundred.

Georgeham, Pickwell and Woolacombe and associated hamlets formed another township. Jordan Haccombe and John Tracy were lords of this township, which was in Shirwell Hundred.

There was a further layer of administration, that of the Church. Under the Saxons the Church was organised into Diosceses headed by a bishop. Each Hundred, especially one based round a royal manor like Braunton had a minster church whose priests served the area. These became parishes; Georgeham was part of Braunton Parish.

The Norman Conquest did not greatly change the system, although the landholders changed. Remaining Saxon thanes lost status, though it is thought they often remained and farmed the same holdings.

It is assumed that the Saxon landholders mentioned in Domesday were very important people, holding vast lands. Ordgar's descendant, Ordwulf, one of whose manors was Croyde still held 20 manors in 1066, in spite of Canute's intervening Danish rule. Edmer (various spellings) who had Ham was another major landholder. They were all important people nationally, so their lands were farmed by others, who, Finberg suggests, became the "villeins" of the Domesday Book. The lands of the main landholders, usually called "tenants in chief" were called Honours, in both Saxon and Norman times.

From Domesday on, we have information on who held the local manors. Reichel provides us with much of it. Risden adds to it.

However, even this is not simple - the area was divided differently, land was aquired/given in marriage, sold, bought, leased, mortgaged, not in major holdings, but piecemeal.. The people who "held" the land did not usually live on it. The names of the actual inhabitants are unknown until they begin to surface in later documents.
Recurrence of names over 600 years suggests a considerable local stability. See the various lists of names in the "Inhabitants" section.

Georgeham, Pickwell

Originally "Ham" at Domesday it was part of Tetbald's lands. Tetbald apparently had no heirs. The village is next heard of when we find part of it quoted as having been held by Galfride de Ham in the time of Henry II (1154 - 1189), from the Honour of Torrington.

From the Bishop of Exeter's registers we learn that in 1241 that Galfride's holding in Ham, Overhamme and Netherhamme was held by Robert de Edington, along with Gratton in High Bray for one fee, from the Honour of Torrington. Robert de Edington was referred to as the "Personne" of Ham, which could imply that he received the Tithes.

In 1241 another half fee in Georgeham was held by Robert de Pidekewill, who also held Pickwell. One of Robert's daughters was married to Mauger de St Aubin who eventually held all Georgeham, Pickwell, Spreacombe, South Hole and South Lobb, as well as other land elsewhere. In 1303 North Hole is included in the estate's land.

In 1261 Georgeham was separated from Braunton Parish and constituted a rectory "by the consolidation of the vicarage of that chapel with the parsonage". Twenty shillings had to be paid yearly to the Dean of Exeter in compensation for loss of church dues from Georgeham. Vicarage dealt with the spiritual side, parsonage with the practical administration of church property, care of the poor, hospitality to travellers, payment to a priest, by the Parson/ personne, funded by the tithes. It suggests that we had a chapel, subordinate to Braunton Parish Church, and that by 1241 the tithes had been going to this area, not Braunton. Since Sir Mauger as Lord of the Manor had the patronage he probably gave land to the church, perhaps the part previously held by Robert de Edington, which became the glebelands. Sir Mauger, or at least, the one who died in 1294 must have lived here at least some of the time since he and his wife had tombs in the church.

In 1346 (Feudal Aids, quoted by Reichel) the Georgeham and Pickwell lands seem to have had four holders; Sir Robert de Crews, Thomas de Merton, John Vautort and John Lercedene to whom land had come by inheritance and marriage from de St Aubin. John Vautort held a half fee in Pickwell, Gratton, Spreacombe and North Hole. Lercedene held Overhamme, Netherhamme and presumably Hamme, since he still had patronage of the rectory. Each of the four holders had to pay a levy of twelve pence!

In 1428 the freeholders Nicholas Carew, Robert Vaucord, Walter Maxworth, Henry Talbut and John Arundel held the half fee John Vautort had held about 100 years earlier.

Between 1443 and 1472 Nicholas Carew, still a descendant of Sir Mauger held Pickwell and Georgeham. The Carew family held this land until Sir Peter Carew sold Pickwell Barton and the barton lands (Barton lands, the Rev. Charles Croslegh tells us were "the lands held by the lord in demesne. The barton is a common Devon name for a large farm. When these lands were converted to copyhold, the several tenements were called "the barton lands""). He sold them to John Newcourt (died 1603). He lived here and is buried in the church. The manors of Georgeham, and Pickwell were sold to Sir John Chichester (i.e. The lordship and lands other than the Barton lands). Sir John took over the patronage of the church.

At some time in the early 17th century Pickwell built a limekiln on the shore now called Vention. It had been realised that the land was lime deficient; yields subsequently improved dramatically.

Pickwell Barton then descended by marriage to the Harris family - who were related to the Chichesters and most other high status families in the region.

Georgeham and the Pickwell lordship were joined with North Buckland, which he, Chichester, had inherited, and continued to be linked with North Buckland until Honour Harris bought it and brought it all back to Pickwell in 1766. The church still owned 33 acres of glebeland in 1727.

Honour died in 1790. One of her inheritors lost money gambling; Darracott, Crowberry and Foot's were sold by 1797/9. By the time Lord Fortescue bought the lands in 1832 they were much depleted, with many farms sold off. This accounts for the difference between the Harris holding shown in the land tax 1791 and Lord Fortescue's in 1839. After Honour's death Pickwell Barton passed through many hands, often being in fact empty.

Lord Fortescue carved out the Pickwell estate (1833 survey) and let it to George Downing, who farmed it, followed by his son and grandson. There was very little property or land in Georgeham itself still belonging to Lord Fortescue by 1839.

The 1901 Census Return shows the Dyers, a large family, farming Pickwell Barton.

In the early 1900s it was sold to Major Montague Style and became a gentleman's residence. When the house burned down he rebuilt it in its current form and also built a farm house for the farmer who actually farmed the land.

He was followed by Colonel Elliott. Both these families lived here for at least part of the time and contributed considerably to the community.

Putsborough

Putsborough may have been part of Domesday Croyde, perhaps the separate virgate held by Ordwulf's sister. It seems to have passed eventually to the Dillons, who inherited part of Croyde from the Flemings. Both families came from the Bratton Fleming area.

From the later 1600s it was held by the Richards family from Kentisbury/ Trentishoe where family members often held church livings.
John Richards died in 1778, leaving much property in Croyde as well as Putsborough. His estate was mostly divided between Roger Heddon and George Horwood, to the latter of whom he was related.

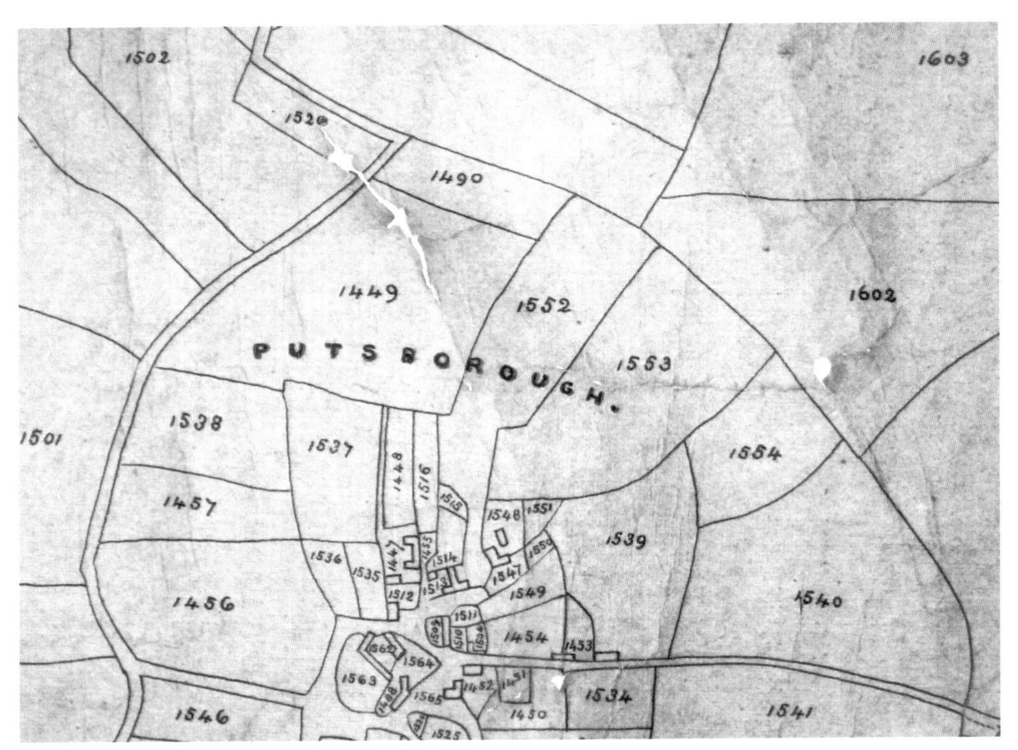

Part of the Putsborough Tithe Map, 1839

The Horwoods kept it until Thomas Horwood died in 1836. However, unlike the Richards, they didn't always live here, because in 1810 Lord Kilmarnock died there. Two of his pictures were bought by a relative, Mr Roberts and descended to Mr Chanter on whose walls they hung in Barnstaple.

The Tithe Map 1839 gives John Dunning as the owner and occupier of Putsborough. The Directories give the Dunning family as major land owners here until 1883, but they were living at Winkleigh by 1856.

It is interesting that Kelly's Directory, 1902, mentions a Major Richard Horwood Dunning of Winkleigh. Were they all related?

The Richards family may have reappeared by 1839 when Mr William Vellacott Richards (also from Kentisbury) was living at Incledon House.

The Directories also show that Francis Alvis was the tenant of the Manor in 1856, followed by Richard Greening Prole, 1878 - 1890, a local man, baptised here. After him came Stuart Coleman in 1897 and Percy Sturdy in 1914. However, the tenants of the Manor do not generally show in the census Returns from 1851. These show only tenant farmers (the Dyer family were here in 1891, before moving to Pickwell before 1901) living in the hamlet, although the 1891 Census caught the ladies of the Gascoigne family living at Putsborough Manor, along with a Belgian maid. Sir Stewart and Lady Robertson bought the manor in 1920 and kept it for 40 years.

The hamlet has been through phases of dereliction, especially in the 1940s. Since then, barns have been rebuilt, houses restored carefully and the hamlet has kept its charm.

North Buckland

North Buckland, a bookland, held directly from the king before 1066 by Bristic Cameron was a small part of William Capra's lands by 1086 of the Honour of Bradninch. The Honour after this reverted to the king, was in the hands of the Traceys, then the Earl of Cornwall, then to Richard Plantagenet in 1243 who was nearly Holy Roman Emperor, lapsed to the king and was granted in 1307 to Piers Gaveston!. Eventually it became part of the lands of the Duke of Cornwall.

These however are just the overlords.

Like Georgeham and Pickwell its subsequent history is complicated. In the Domesday book it is shown as a larger holding than Georgeham.

In 1303, Hugh de Valletort held a half fee; in 1328 part of it was rented out to de Campo Arnulfi (Champernoun) whose family held it until 1420. Its lands at this point included parts of Darracott. John Champernoun of Buckland Dinham still held them in 1543.

In 1543 Sir Richard Eggscombe sold the manor to Alexander Wode of North Tawton (enrolled Deed no. 204).

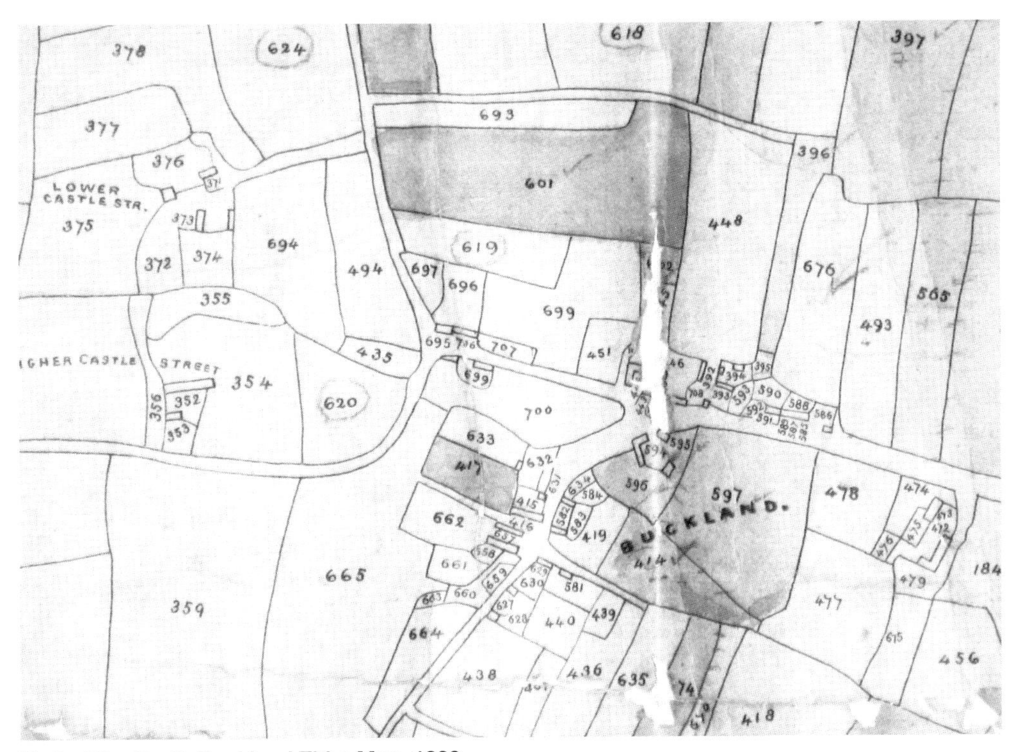

Part of the North Buckland Tithe Map, 1839

Rev. Charles Croslegh, vicar of Bradninch, in his book "Bradninch" gives a list of tenants of the Honour. These included, in 1650, the heirs of Castle, Buckland Dinham; Sir John Chichester, Bart., the manor of Buckland Dinham; John Wood, gent, heir of lands in "Bocland (sic); Dillon, land in Buckland Dinham.

In 1441 John Arundel held part of North Buckland, then it passed through various hands until 1670 when John Chichester held it, by inheritance, along with Pickwell and Georgeham. He sold it in 1704 to George Buck who kept it until 1766. At this stage, Mr Buck's manor included a large part of Georgeham, with the church in the middle. Lord Fortescue bought it all in 1832. By 1839 much of it had been bought by the mysterious "Flood and Mules", possibly local land speculators.

Parts of the old Buck estate, some of Rock Hill, including the Rock public house, were paying rent some time later to Buckland Denham estate, Denham Farm serving as the estate office. Otherwise, North Buckland by this time was a group of farms.

The 1905 OS map shows the site of a Manor House, and also the site of the chapel of St Anthony, opposite Gibb's Farm. Mr Stevenson Balfour did not find a mention of a license for this in the Bishops of Exeters' registers, although licenses were granted to Spreacombe, Pickwell, Croyde and Hole. It is therefore possible that the Buckland chapel predated the creation of the parish in 1261. The field identified as the site for this chapel was called Chapel Field on the Tithe Map, and unlike others in Buckland has a number relating to old landholding , including the graveyard, in Georgeham.

Buckland Dinham/Dynham/Denham

The reason for it being called Buckland Dinham/Denham is obscure. Although there is a mention of Buckland Dinham in Georgeham in 1259 (the 1424 Calender Patent Rolls suggest this was actually Buckland Dinham in Somerset) and the name was perpetuated in official records thereafter. Yet there is no record of any of the Dinham family being connected with this area until the 15th century, and then only by marriage. The Dinhams did indeed hold Hartland and were an important family. While it is possible that they were connected with Buckland in the turbulent times of William II (Rufus) and later of John it is surprising that no record of this connection survives. They owned Buckland Dinham in Somerset. It seems probable that an early confusion occurred and was copied by later officials. (If the famous map maker, Ogilby, could put Ford Abbey at Forda, just because it sounds the same and they're both somewhere in the west, anything is possible). Later, perhaps people found it useful to keep the Buckland Denham name to distinguish it from Buckland in Braunton.

Further confusion exists because Thomas Westcote , mid 1600s and James Davidson in 1832 describe the armory in the church; the first before the 1760 restoration, the latter before the Victorian one. Mr Balfour suggested that the arms were displayed on shields painted on the galleries. Gregory Chichester of Pickwell had built a gallery, and on it were the arms of Bouchier, Carew, Chichester, Talbot, Batcombe, Cridhoe, Cridwell, and Gifford.

John Harris pulled down this gallery and replaced it. Honour Harris applied for permission to build a second gallery. They appear to have followed Gregory Chichester's habit of decorating the galleries with shields - of anyone related to them by marriage. Davidson records arms of Chichester, Newcourt, Harris, Dinham impaling Gwyn (or Herbert more likely as John Harris was married to Dorothy Herbert), Newton, Talbot and Noble.

Curiously, the arms imputed to Dinham are not those of the Hartland branch. Still in the church at Georgeham, in the Pickwell Chapel, is a sculpted shield with the arms of Harris, quarterly of eight; Harris, de Esse/Ash, Dinham, Wortham, Westmanton, Byefied, Prideaux, Harris. This time the Dinham arms are those of the Hartland family - gules, four fusils in fess ermine.

The name Buckland Dynham continued in use until 1777 at least, because in that year, on 6th October, John and William Badcock had tenements in Buckland Dynham, Georgeham for sale in the Sherbourne and Yeovil Mercury. They may not have been successful in their attempts to sell since, in 1839 John Badcock, himself, held Gibbs Farm, 53 acres. James had tenants in North Buckland Cottages and another farm of 29 acres.

The same Tithe Apportionments show that Denham Farm had 69 acres, making it the largest of the North Buckland holdings. John Barnes was at Broadgate with 56 acres.

Darracott

Darracott is something of a mystery. In the Assize Rolls of 1302 it is called Dodecote. Later, in 1501 it is called Doddecot, and could have been part of the holding of Doda, who held Saunton pre 1066. It is surprising that the hamlet kept its name from pre Conquest times, and yet, unlike Lobb is not mentioned in Domesday.

It had, according to Mr Balfour, two main farms and one other. Both main farms burned down in the early 20th century and were rebuilt.

In 1818 Robert Hole of Georgeham owned land there; the Deanes farmed there. We know that the farm belonging to Honour Harris (Pickwell) was sold by her inheritor in the 1790s.

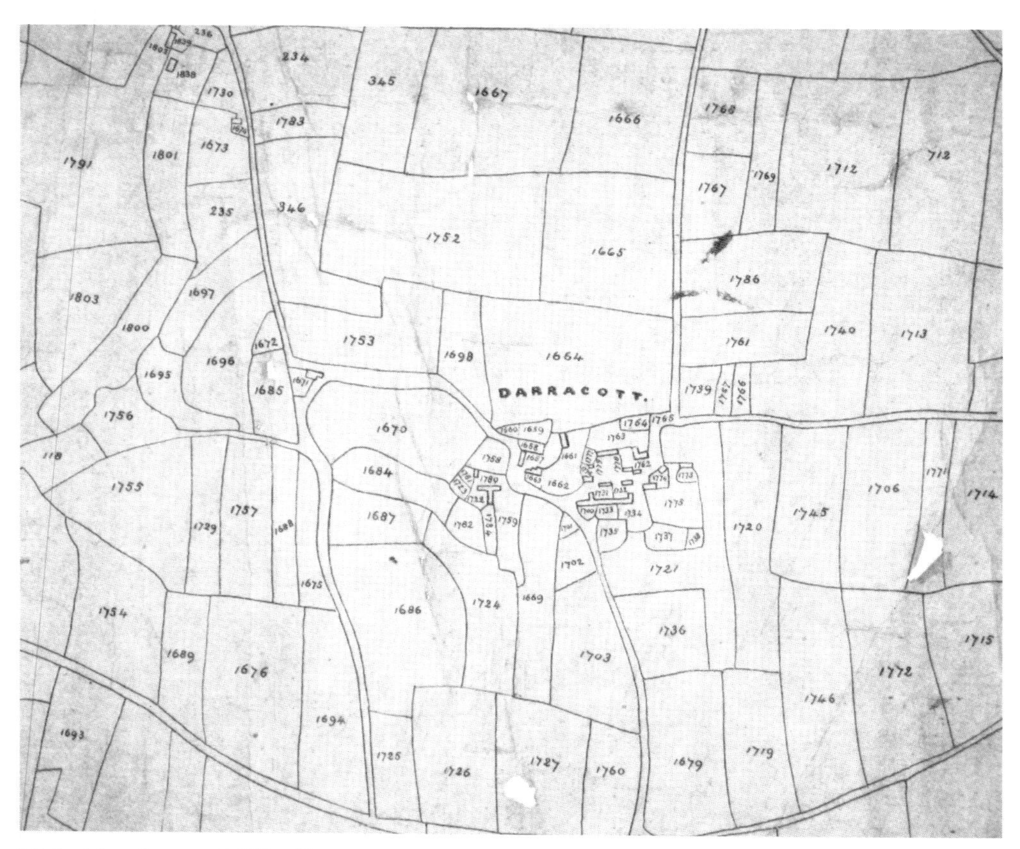

Part of the Darracott Tithe Map

Land in Darracott had been given to fund Braunton Free School (Chaloners) and from 1641 twenty-one acres funded the Litchden Almshouses in Barnstaple.

In 1979 there was a sale of 51 acres on behalf of the Barnstaple Municipal Charities and Mrs K E Hancock.

Land Use

According to Westcote, Tacitus, in the first century said that it was easier to get the people to fight and risk wounds than to manure the fields and that they felt it unmanly to get by sweat and toil what you could just as easily get by shedding blood.

William of Malmsbury, Westcote continues, said that Devon yielded scarcely any grain but oats and pulse, and that coarse and slender.

However, the Saxons had come to farm, whatever the problems and habits of the Britons.
Georgeham has no obvious survival of the strip farming of a huge field which is seen on the Braunton Great Field. Some areas in Croyde and North Buckland look as though they had strips but that they were subsequently hedged - more use for keeping cattle.

Westcote at the beginning of the 16th century noted that the soil needed a lot of manurance and that seaweed was used as well as sand (sand here is lime rich because much of it is formed from shells). He speaks too of a very common method of removing turf, burning it and using the ashes as fertiliser. He also mentions the very new use of lime. In later years, he says, orchards have been much enlarged and all kinds of fruit produced. Much cider was made.

He comments that the land is enclosed "with strange hedges, fences and dykes" good for providing shelter for cattle and sheep, also enabling them to be moved frequently to fresh pasture. Shepherds and cowherds did not need to stay with them.

Furthermore, in maintaining their hedges they "have sufficient fuel for their fires all year long". Just as well as there was little woodland left. Flowers usually associated with woodland here grow in banks and hedges, primroses, bluebells, violets.

W G Hoskins comments that in the 16th century large areas were taken into cultivation - often given names like "Barton Park" or "South Park" but that these were subsequently divided into smaller units with banks and hedges. These fields are reasonably regular in shape. There was further enclosure later. Pickwell Down and Saunton Down are shown as open land on Ogilby's map c. 1675, and the former seems still to be open land on the Pickwell estate map of 1833.

Risdon, more or less contemporary with Westcote was proud of the Devon cattle and sheep, and tough horses "which can endure any hardships in other shires".

Corn, he said, was plentiful, wheat, barley, rye, oats, pulses, vetches, "as well for navigation as for the sustenance of the inhabitants". Trees, he says were lacking, but, like Westcote, comments on the good variety of fruit trees and the prevalence of cider.

He points out that because of the soil , much work and toil are needed. He was very appreciative of the introduction of lime to the land. "And of late , a new invention hath sprung up… by burning lime and incorporating it for a season with earth and then spread on the arable land, hath produced a plentiful increase of all sorts of grain where formerly such never grew in any living man's memory". (This lime, apparently slaked, was carried round the area in the panniers of strings of pack ponies.)

J.T. who wrote a commentary for the 1810 edition of Risdon's book was a little more critical, as the fields spread with lime and made fertile, "are again made barren by the practice of taking crop after crop of corn". Other parts of the country, he said, had made greater progress in agriculture. Devon generally had lagged behind. The cider orchards were decaying.

One reason for this, he suggests, was the way the land was held. Rent, in Risdon's time was low, tenants had enough to live on merrily, the three lifetime leases gave no incentive to improve the land. In 1810 this system was going out of use, to be replaced with short leases, discouraging expensive operations and rents too high to make investment in the land possible.

The farm houses, he continues, are in an appalling state - "generally bad and unfit for a respectable tenancy" and the farms themselves too small to attract ambitious tenants.

However, in 1810 the cattle were flourishing and most were a "fine dark red" At least JT says that the county in general was no longer "barren and full of brakes and briers" as Risdon reported, but full of beauty and fertility.

Sadly though, raw products, wool, manganese, were sent away for processing, so others made more profit.

How far Georgeham fitted into the general pattern it is difficult to say. Pickwell appears to have been run as a successful estate by the Harris family, and before. Its limekiln is surely a mark of progress, but by the 18th century much of the land otherwise seems to have been in the hands of small tenant farmers.

Cattle here, about 1755 are recorded in Dean Milles' survey as being "mostly black" but "handsome all" and were sent to markets at Barnstaple, South Molton and Fremmington.
A lot of land in the centre of the village seems to have been orchard.

Farmer owners, yeomen, as one of the Directories calls them are in evidence by 1840, but often the land was held in very small parcels and well scattered.

In the early 20th century some holdings were very small, making for barely subsistence farming, with people owning just 2 or 3 cows. The small fields, Ben Isaac told me, were sometimes worked, like an allotment, with fork and spade, by just one man.

The Tithe Map gives us a view of land use in1839/40. Please see the section "The Tithe Map" later.

There has been a considerable shift in land use since 1839 when 2862 acres were listed as "arable" and 158 acres "meadow" or "pasture". Today about half of the land is arable, the rest pasture for sheep and cattle.

On the estate map for Pickwell, 1833, there is a field listed as "Vineyard". Mr Balfour noted that one form of the name of Winners/ Winnard Hill in Georgeham is Vineyard Hill. Both these are south facing and free draining. Not unsuitable.

The really major change between the 1920s and 1960s was the increasing mechanisation of farming. Changing from horse power to tractors not only meant that work could be done faster, but also that people were not needed to look after the horses. Mechanised hedging, ploughing, planting and harvesting needed far fewer farm workers. The result was that instead of employing twenty people perhaps just two extra hands were needed. Agriculture was no longer a major employer. People had to seek employment elsewhere

However, the demand for home produced food in the Second World War, and agricultural subsidies (to prevent us again relying on imported food) afterwards gave enormous encouragement to energetic farming. Larger farming units were formed by owner occupiers. Production and prosperity increased.

In 2008, we still have Foote farm in the village centre although now it only has sheep. North Hole has a large dairy herd. South Hole and Incledon are mixed farms as is the large farm at Pickwell and another at North Buckland.

Houses

The old houses are cob built and were thatched - some still are. It is unlikely that many, if any at all, predate the 17th century. In many cases the main beams and lintels are salvaged ships timbers. Since cob is easily available and timber can be reused it is difficult to say exactly when a house was built or altered. Sometimes a neat 18th century façade is backed by a much older structure with rougher cob, thicker walls and small windows. Slate roofs became common in the 19th century and the Old Manse, built as a chapel and houses of the same period are built of local stone - sometimes shillet, as the local builders call it somewhat disparagingly. Lime ash floors were laid directly on the rock; foundations were minimal.

Since most of the houses are now faced and plastered it is not easy to see what they are made of. Perhaps this explains the great interest shown in any building work!

The larger houses in the village are early 19th century. Pickwell was rebuilt in the early 20th century after a fire. Putsborough Manor is much older, but has been much altered and modernised.

Tithe Map 1839/40

From Saxon times Tithes had been paid. In theory they were collected and paid to the Rector of a parish for the maintenance of the church, payment for a priest, or offering hospitality. In practice the Rector didn't always live in the parish and the Tithes were just a useful income. The tithes were often paid in kind and had to be converted to cash.

By the 1830s it was felt that this was a rather inconvenient way of doing things and furthermore it was greatly resented.

In 1836 the Tithes Commutation Act was passed, which required all tithes to be paid in cash. Commissioners were appointed to negotiate land values in each parish.

For Georgeham, the process was not complete until 1840 when a copy had been made of the original map for local use. This copy is now in the North Devon Records Office in Barnstaple. It was obviously used as some areas are

Part of the Georgeham Tithe Map, 1839

shaded in green and some plot numbers have had circles drawn round them. Written at the bottom of the map is -

"We the undersigned Commissioners for England and Wales do hereby certify this to be a copy of the map or plan referred to in the Apportionment of the Rent Charges in lieu of Tithes in the Parish of Georgeham in the County of Devon"

The map shows all the fields and houses, the latter in red on the original map, which were in existence at the time it was made. With the map one finds also the Apportionments which give information on ownership, tenants and land usage.

There are 1844 entries on the Georgeham map and Apportionments, of which the houses account for 240 entries, the fields 1604.

These extracts are taken from the Apportionment of the Rent Charge in lieu of Tithes in the Parish of Georgeham in the County of Devon.

"Know all men by these presents that I George Louis having been duly appointed and sworn as an assistant Tithe Commissioner according to the provisions of the Commutation of Tithes in England and Wales and having been also duly appointed to ascertain and award the Total to be paid by way of Rent Charge instead of Tithes of the Parish of Georgeham in the County of Devon do hereby award as follows that is to say whereas I have held divers meetings in the said parish touching the matter aforesaid of which meetings due notice was given for the information of the Landowners and Titheowners of the said Parish."

The Commissioner found that the three mills, Manor Mill, Heddon Mill and Hole Mill already paid cash, 3s 4d for the Manor Mill, and 2s for each of the others.

He found also that other goods in kind had been replaced by cash, at a rate previously agreed in the parish, i.e. 1s for a colt, 6d for a calf, 1d for the milk of a cow, ¼d for the milk of a ewe and 1d for a herb garden.
There was also a previous arrangement for the tithing of lambs.

The Commissioner continued "... I find that the estimated quantity in statute measure of all lands of the said parish which are subject to payment of Tithes amounts to:

> 3496 acres 3 roods 10 perches which are cultivated as follows -
> 2862 acres 3 roods 39 perches as arable land
> 107 acres 1 rood 15 perches as meadow
> 41 acres 1 rood as pasture
> 62 acres 3 roods as woodlands
> 38 acres 3 roods 16 perches as orchard and gardens
> 373 acres 2 roods 20 perches as common lands"

The cash for Tithes conversion was the average value of the Tithe over the last seven years.

The Commissioner felt, however, that here the average value of the Tithes for the last seven years was "not a fair sum" and used instructions of the Act of Parliament as well as the seven year average. He ascertained that the Rector of the Parish was entitled to all the Tithes and awarded the annual sum of £500 by way of Rent Charge and a further £7 10s as a Rent Charge on the Glebe Lands.

It was signed by George Louis and dated 12th April 1839.

The Valuer was Thomas Lock of Instow who duly apportioned the Rent Charge as... £ 500 10s.

The price of wheat, barley and oats per bushel was given:

Wheat	7s ¼d
Barley	3s 11 ½d
Oats	2s 9d

Each field, plot, house, road and bit of waste land was given a number on the map.

In the Apportionments the name of the owner, occupier, acreage, and use were given. The values of each were given in a separate section.

The numbering of the plots reflects the owners to a certain extent, but also areas. The numbers 1787 - 1844 are interesting as they involve several different owners in various areas; 1844 is the Chapel Field at North Buckland.

Nothing like the Tithe survey and Apportionments was ever attempted again. Previously, the only obvious comparable survey was the Domesday Book.

However, in 1909/10 the Finance Act included provision for taxing any future increase in the value of land from a baseline in 1909. All land owned in England and Wales was surveyed. This survey was undertaken by District Valuation Offices of the Commissioners of the Inland Revenue. Maps were made and Field Books compiled, listing owners, their land and its value. These books are sometimes referred to as "Domesday" books.

A copy of the Field Book for Georgeham is in the North Devon Records Office, but the maps are only available in London. The valuer was Mr Fowler from Darracott.

The information from the maps and books is much used to establish the existence of Rights of Way and in particular of vehicular rights of way. People generally are not aware of the Field Books unless, as Georgeham was, they are involved with problems with rights of way. The Planning Inspectorate's current website suggests that caution is needed in interpreting the evidence gained from this source.

Mining in the Area

Although there were mines at North Buckland and at Spreacombe no mention has been found of any miners living in Georgeham, or in the Census area.

There is no mention of mines in the 1839/40 Tithe information.

However, Mr Balfour was aware of the existence of the mines and his interest was widely known. In 1978 he was in contact with J F Claughton who had researched these mines, among others, and kindly sent the information to Mr Balfour. He was keen that the information should be published and left it with Mr and Mrs Mounteney. A picture of miners at Spreacombe was included in the 1989 version of Mr Balfour's book, but very little information.

From "Mining In The Parish Of Georgeham", by Mr P F Claughton, Williamson Terrace, Llanwym, Haverfordwest.

"Although this parish has a long and interesting history there is no evidence of the exploitation of its mineral deposits until the second half of the 19th century. These deposits, composed of north-south crosscourses filled with brecciated country rock cemented with the oxides of iron and manganese, haematite and psilomelane, lie at the western end of a series found in rock of the Pickwell Down Beds (Upper Devonian) running across North Devon from Molland in the east. At Molland and North Molton the iron and manganese are associated with copper. However, there is no evidence of this occurring at Georgeham, although it has been suggested in the past that a trial in depth be made at Spreacombe to test the possibility. **(1)**

The first evidence of exploitation comes in 1861 when the North Buckland Mine (NGR SS 492.404) was being worked, possibly by the Plymouth Iron Co. of Merthyr Tydfil, who were operating mines in the parishes of Shirwell and Bratton Fleming at that time. It is evident that the mine was at work for the majority of the year, for there was an accident in part of the mine which had been abandoned earlier in the year. **(2)** Reference to the Tithe Award of 1839, and other documents, provide no indication of mineral working at any earlier date.

It was another nine years before there was any further activity, when it was reported in the Mining Journal that a company with a capital of £50,000 was to be formed to raise iron ore on the estate of Mr Riddell at Spreacombe. Some ore had been raised in 1870, probably at the mine known later as Spreacombe Mine (NGR SS 478.413) **(3)**. This company does not appear to have come to anything as by 1872 the mine was in the hands of the Ynyscedwyn Iron, Steel and Coal Co.. By this time there were at least two other iron mines in operation in the parish; the North Buckland Mine having been reopened by a Mr Bagshott, and by July 1872 was down to a depth of nearly 800 feet; another mine, referred to as being "near Georgeham" was being worked by a Mr Ellis. This was probably at Roadway Corner (NGR SS 466.423), actually in Mortehoe parish, where a shaft was situated just south of the road junction and ore has been ploughed up in the field to the west. Additionally, prospecting was being carried out for iron and manganese on the Pickwell Manor estate under license granted to Robert Smith by Earl Fortescue. This latter probably resulted in the small trial working on the western edge of Pickwell Down, 500 yards north of the manor, where a narrow iron vein can be traced in an adjacent quarry and traces of the manganese referred to by De la Beche in 1839 can be seen in the rocks exposed on the beach north of Vention. **(4)**.

Spreacombe was, however, the major concern in the area, as indicated by the Parish Council, who in 1875 rated the mine at gross £43, rateable £40, whereas North Buckland was only £20, rateable £19. **(5)**

Held by Ynyscedwyn, a company operating blast furnaces in the parish of Ystradgynlais, Breconshire, this mine was being opened up on the south side of the lane from Oxford Cross to Spreacombe Bridge. In 1872, under the management of Capt. Keast, two shafts had been sunk on the hillside and an adit driven south from the lane. Workings had been taken below adit level but were troubled by water during wet weather as no pumping machinery had been installed. Iron ore was being produced at this date, but the amount is not recorded. **(6)**. By 1877 the low price of iron and the reorganisation of the Tynysedwyn Co. had caused the closure of the mine after producing 654 tons of brown haematite, valued at £422. **(7)**

The North Buckland Mine which had passed into the hands of D Cameron Park in 1874 without any recorded output, was again at work in 1882 under a lease granted to J N Anthony (of Combe Martin Umber Mines) and P Furlong, but although three miners were employed there was still no recorded output. **(8)**.

In 1887 negotiations were in progress for the reopening of the Spreacombe Mine, a lease of which had been granted in May 1886 to a Mr Peverill, of St Austell by Mr Ridell, at a royalty of 6d per ton of iron ore. This lease was assigned to persons connected with the Dowlais Iron Co. in May of that year and it was their intention to connect the mine with the Barnstaple and Ilfracombe Railway by means of a tramway. **(9)** However, their plans do not seem to have materialised, for no tramway was built and within a month the mine was in the hands of G P Jay who, with the Spreacombe Mining Syndicate opened up the mine for manganese and iron. The former was extracted from an open-cast working to the north of a lane on the site of what is now a SWEB sub-station; a contemporary photograph shows no less than 34 men and boys employed on this task, but surprisingly, there is no recorded output.

Miners at Spreacombe

In March 1888 a limited company, The Spreacombe Vall Mine Ltd. **(10)** was formed to take over from the syndicate.. A deep adit , commencing as a short crosscut, was driven from Mines Plantation, presumably to counter the water problems experienced by the Ynyscedwin Co., and shafts were sunk to the north of the lane in addition to extending the workings under the hill to the south. A treatment plant was erected at the western end of the Mines Plantation where the iron ore was crushed and sorted into two grades, the fines being sold for use in rust resistant paint, while the coarse ore was shipped to South Wales, some to be used as a purifier in gas works. The output totalled only 125 tons before the mine closed in 1890, and this was shipped out via Vellator Quay at Braunton, no use being made of the railway.

This closure did not mark the end for the mines, for with the outbreak of the First World War and the emphasis on home production of minerals they were reopened. Spreacombe was re-equipped, an adit was driven west from the hillside at NGR SS 4945 4019, north of Heddon Mill, to try the veins of the North Buckland Mine and numerous trial pits were dug throughout the area, but the ore found could not be economically worked.

Since that date the mines have lain unnoticed by the majority of people. Part of the Spreacombe site was quarried away during the Second World War and is now occupied by a SWEB sub-station. Workings at both Spreacombe and North Buckland can still be entered, but reveal little of interest, although the deep adit at Spreacombe has been entered by a local diver, despite the large amount of water present, and an old wagon discovered.

These workings provide an example of what was basically an un-economical ore deposit to which adventurers were attracted by the prevailing high price of the metal, only to be disappointed when the price fell."

References:

1) Dines 1956, "Metalliferous Mining Region of South West England", p. 759; these veins are counter to the iron veins associated with the Stockland and Fullabrook mines to the east, which are east-west.

2) North Devon Journal 7/11/1861; The Plymouth Iron Co. surrenders their lease of mines on the Chichester estates at Shirwell and Bratton Fleming in 1866.

3) Mining Jounal 2/4/1870

4) Ilfracombe Chronicle 20/7/1872; The lease granted to Robert Smith, who had been the agent to the Exmoor estate during iron working by the Dowlais Co. covered all Earl Fortescue's land in the parish of Georgeham, excluding that granted to Mr Bagshott, who had taken a mineral license of Pickwell Wood, later known as South Wood, to the north of the North Buckland Mine. Prospecting was carried on until 1875, but in 1876 a fresh license was granted to Captain Pope of Fullabrook Mine. Devon Record Office D1262M/E25/7.

5) Georgeham Vestry Minute Book 13/4/1875; information kindly supplied by Mr Balfour of Georgeham. In the Minute Book, Spreacombe is referred to as Buckland Mine causing some confusion, but this was clarified by the naming of the owner as Mr Hende (Hendre) which linked it with the Ynyscedwyn Co.

6) Ilfracombe Chronicle 20/7/1872.

7) Mineral Statistics Geol. Survey and Home Office; the company agent during this period was George Boyle who combined this with farming at North Buckland.

8) Reports of H M Inspector of Mines, South Western District.

9) Glamorgan Record Office D/DG B Box 8

10) Registered 22/3/1888 with a nominal capital of £30,000 in £1 shares, of which 14, 504 had been taken by 3/8/1888 with a call of 18s on each. Offices at 35 Coleman St. London. Public Record Office BT 31.

Roads

Most roads connecting villages and settlements were in place by the 10th century. Townships had to work together. Representatives had to attend the meetings of the Hundred. For Georgeham this was Braunton, but Pickwell was in Shirwell Hundred.

The dead had to be taken to the parish church for burial. Before 1261 that meant Braunton, after that, Georgeham.

The old track logged by Ogilby c. 1675, Ilfracombe - Georgeham - Bideford and beyond may be older. It doesn't link settlements in any obvious way.

W G Hoskins in "*The making of the English Landscape*" remarks that roads often marked boundaries, especially those with banks and hedges at each side. Many of our roads are of this type.

Where a road crossed open down land, when the open land was enclosed, the track had to be banked/hedged.

There were laws saying how wide a road should be, according to its purpose, but here , the narrow, deep tracks were mostly retained. They were described at intervals between the 16th and 19th centuries as being appallingly muddy, stony, difficult for horse and foot and unsuitable for wheeled vehicles.

Maintenance of the highways (roads/tracks that went somewhere) was first the duty of the Manor, then of the church parish from the late 16th century, then from 1894 of the civil parish. After that it was taken over by the District and County Councils. The parish paid local people for stone from the quarries and others to repair the roads with the broken stones. Local roads were not dressed with tarmac until well into the 20th century.

When the roads were taken over by the District and County Councils problems arose. When the RDC took over it was supposed to list all public highways, roads, tracks or footpaths which were repaired at public expense. There were inevitably many arguments.

Long Lane was a case in point. The Georgeham/Braunton parish boundary runs along the middle of it. Georgeham parish denied all knowledge of it. Braunton after energetic representation from those farmers who might use it and/or have to repair it, thought it might possibly have previously repaired it. The question of whether or not it was a public highway, thus repaired at public expense rumbled on until a Public Inquiry in 2005 decided that on balance it probably was a public road. This opened it up to public vehicular traffic - which found itself at a dead end at a T-junction with a bridleway!

One reason for the poor state of Devon's roads was that, according to Risdon's commentator in 1810, the local stone was either impossibly hard, or alternatively rather soft and easily ground down into mud. If of course your road was down to bedrock, like Mill lane in Croyde, it just wore down a bit further and the loose bits washed down to make mud somewhere else. If you factor in the rapid growth of vegetation here in already narrow lanes it is easy to see why road maintenance was such a nightmare.

From the village, the road to Putsborough Beach is labelled on a 1690 map as "Ye King's Highway". The road from Higher Ham to Oxford Cross appears incomplete on a 1721 map. The 1839 Tithe map shows that, complete by then, it crossed obvious field boundaries. The Oxford Cross to Bye Cross route seems to have been the older route. From there it went down Rock Hill, then down Back Lane which accounts for the properties on Rock Hill being split by the current road. Within the village the Tithe map seems to show that there were ways round and between houses. They weren't each fenced into a little plot.

The Pickwell estate map 1833 shows no road from Oxford Cross to Roadway. The 1904 OS map shows the approach road to Pickwell from the Putsborough Road went straight to the Manor. The road which now swings right and then left round the Manor did not exist.

In fact, the road from the Putsborough Road to Pickwell was not a public road until some time between 1905 and 1928. Until the 1960s it had an impressive stone pillar on each side. On one map, Mr Balfour has called this road Whitegate Hill, which suggests that it was in fact gated.

Local landowners had belonged, in the mid 18th century, to the Barnstaple

Turnpike Trust and had an interest in improving most roads. Many of the used roads were improved slowly for use by horse and cart. It is worth remembering though that the first mail coach to Barnstaple was in 1827 and the current Barnstaple to Braunton road dates from 1830, after the building of the bridge over the River Yeo. Previously Pilton Bridge was used, and the Old Barnstaple Road.

Furthermore, with no route from Oxford Cross to Roadway, according to the Pickwell map, the route to Ilfracombe went down Mains Down Lane and then, either by the track to Roadway or straight on up Hartnolls lane. Mostly very muddy, and not very suitable for carts. Fortunately most people walked, some had horses. Apparently the quickest route from Mortehoe to Georgeham was via the beach.

The road to Braunton is mostly on higher ground. Darracott must have presented problems - though the 1st edition OS maps show two routes from Darracott to Lobb Stile. Bye Cross itself is a damp corner. However, Mr Isaac notes that farmers used to have drains through the banks to drain the water off the road.

In 1895 there were complaints at the Parish Council meeting that the road from Forda to Lobb Stile (Old or Hole Cleave Road) was much too narrow for convenience. Widening it was discussed by the Parish Council. Before the Saunton Road was opened in 1906 this was the route by which carts went from Croyde to Braunton. And there were tales, a current Croyde resident told me, of a ghostly lady who sat on the stile knitting, causing grief to carters on their way home from a successful visit to market. Hardly the fault of the road though!

Georgeham and the Sea

Georgeham old village is completely hidden from the sea. However, the sea is not so far away and villagers' lives have not escaped its influence.

Anyone standing on the hills around at any time would have been able to see any trading, raiding or naval vessels in the area.

In Roman times they could have watched ships of the Roman navy rounding the Promontory of Hercules and patrolling the Bristol Channel on the look out for possible invaders or pirates intercepting trading vessels. Perhaps somebody saw the Celtic missionary saints arriving in their little boats, or coming ashore from a trader. The Bristol Channel was a busy place!

There is a story that Vikings landed on the beach and that determined locals fought them on the terraces below Pickwell and drove them off. There was a Viking base on Lundy and it would certainly be surprising if their ships weren't seen from time to time.

The Anglo-Saxon Chronicle tells us that in 1069 "came Harold's sons from Ireland at midsummer with sixty-four ships into the mouth of the Taw…" No doubt they were seen too.

In 1167 one of the Sir Maugers de St Aubyn - a family connected with Pickwell, although they had other lands locally - was fined one half mark for seizing a wreck.

Sand from the beaches, having a high shell content, was used as a fertiliser on the land, which is lime deficient in this area. The road down to the beach was labelled, on a 1690 map as "Ye King's Highway", and where roads met the sands one often sees "Sand Gate", written on the map, implying a right of way to the usually crown land of the beach. Normally, the beaches below median high water belong to the crown, as does anything washed up from a wreck. Hence Sir Mauger's fine!

From the early 16th century however limekilns were built, limestone burned and the lime subsequently put on to the land, possibly mixed with soil or dung. The limekiln on Putsborough Beach belonged to Pickwell, whose owner at the time referred to it as his New Invention. Hence, Vention.

The limestone was brought in by boat at high tide and dropped over on to the beach, for collection at lower tide. At the same time as bringing limestone there was the suggestion that the lime boats met French boats in the Bristol Channel and picked up brandy and other desirable goods for untaxed delivery! It is said that the Coastal Path owes its existence to the Customs Officers who had to patrol the coastline.

From the 14th to the 16th century watchers might have seen the pirates who lived at intervals on Lundy, or possibly the Corsair slavers who raided all up the south and west coasts as far as Iceland.

In general, it would have been a good idea to keep watch on the sea. Early warning would have allowed villagers to disappear with their goods. In fact, watch was still being kept during the Napoleonic War when sighting a French ship meant calling out the militia. A coastal watch was also kept during the two World Wars.

In 1700 an enterprising villager from Georgeham, Mr Nutt, obtained a license from the owner of Saunton Court allowing him to collect samphire, lobsters etc from Crow Point to Down End - all of which foreshore belonged to Saunton.

On a less happy note one of the most frequent links between Georgeham and the sea was the retrieval and burial of those drowned at sea whose bodies washed up at Croyde or Putsborough. It was a parish duty. When HMS Weazle was wrecked off Baggy many of her crew were buried in the churchyard here. Some, including the surgeon, are buried in Braunton. Burials of those washed ashore are recorded all through the parish Register of Burials.

The wreck of the Weazle also gives us a wonderful insight into what happened after a wreck. The locals descended in force and the local official, P. R.Webber JP, had to organise the overseeing of anything washed up, very fast. Two villagers from Croyde were fined for trespassing in their eagerness to acquire goods. A Mr Smith from Croyde was put in charge and people were paid for their time and use of their carts to collect all the goods, which were then auctioned. Timber for building was in short supply locally so anything rescued from the sea was in great demand. The rector of Georgeham bought part of the foremast of the Weasel and other bits and pieces. Ships timbers have often been reused in the cottages as lintels, and at least once as a main beam.

By the 20th century tourists were arriving to holiday at the seaside. It was found necessary to provide lifesaving equipment at Croyde because the beaches were beginning to be used for pleasure, families walking down to the sea for the day, children playng in the pools. It has been suggested that the real village children did not go playing on the beach, possibly because they were busy at home.

In other ways the beach was a resource for villagers. Sand could be collected by local builders and used, but not until it had been left in a heap for the rain to wash at least some of the salt out of it.

Collecting driftwood and seaweed was another possibility. Some locals still collect laver from the rocks.

Henry Williamson records an old lady who used to go down with a pram, collecting anything that might be useful. R.V. Thompson in "Home in Ham" tells of the younger male villagers who used to take the village long net down to the beach at low tide on summer evenings, catching fish which they sold round the village. The net used to dry at the back of the cottages now known as Rockcliff. Rev. David Rudman said that the net was still around (in his attic), but that nobody was inclined to use it. Braunton men used the same system at Saunton beach. A few years ago a team tried to do the same at Croyde, but sadly this resulted in a fatality. Apart from the use of the long net there is no record of organised fishing by the villagers.

From the 1950s onwards the beach has been a magnet for summer visitors. Literally thousands of people enjoy it; families with children poking in the rock pools; older children playing rounders or with Frisbees; people who walk or run across to Woolacombe. Many of the visitors stayed in the village, with relatives, in Bed and Breakfast accommodation, in caravans and tents on campsites, bringing in some welcome cash. By 2000 surfing had become very popular; hoards of young people descending to enjoy the sport on the local beaches (and pubs). This too has provided a boost to the economy.

Out of season the beach still forms an important area for locals to relax, take exercise, walk dogs, and enjoy the fabulous scenery. When the tide goes out, everything is left pristine and the pools are sparkling clear,. Magic.

And Now...

It will be obvious that this book is simply a step in the recording of the history of Georgeham and hamlets. There are many areas that need further research. The farms and houses have their own stories and it would be good to have to have more information on agriculture since 1940.

Families will have their own records and photographs and a social history could be built up. Hopefully people with deeds, records and photographs will keep them safe. Some have been loaned for exhibitions and presumably reclaimed.

There is no central repository for this material apart from the North Devon Records Office but it would be an excellent project at least to keep in the village a record of what is available.

The North Devon Records Office above the Library in Barnstaple has a growing list of deeds, maps etc. for Georgeham, Croyde and hamlets. This can be mined for information. They also have Census Returns 1841 - 1901, Parish Registers, Parish Council and Georgeham Parish Institute Minutes, the Tithe Map and Apportionments, some estate maps, Mr Stevenson-Balfour's notes and book collection, as well as a wide range of background information.

Appendix 1: Timeline

	National	*Local*
500 AD		St. Brannock in Braunton
800		Saxons dominate area
924	ATHELSTANE	
957	EDGAR	Ordgar, Duke of Devon, held Croyde
988		Viking raids on Devon, Wales, Somerset
1014	CANUTE King of Denmark and England	
1042	EDWARD The Confessor	Ulf held Pickwell Etmar held Georgeham, Spreacombe and Saunton.
1066	HAROLD (Briefly)	
1066	WILLIAM I (The Conqueror)	Bishop of Coutances held Pickwell Theobald Fitz Bernier held Georgeham
1087	WILLIAM II (Rufus)	
1096	First Crusade	
1100	HENRY I	
1135	STEPHEN and MATILDA Civil war	The de St Aubin family held Pickwell and Georgeham
1154	HENRY II Thomas a Becket	**1167** there was a Galfride de Ham **1186** there was a Reinald de Pidkerville
1189	RICHARD I	
1199	JOHN	
1215	Magna Carta	
1216	HENRY III	**1231** there was a Robert de Edington in Ham **1249** Robert de Pideswill was granted Pickwell by Sir Mauger de St Aubin.
1261		Georgeham church was consolidated and became an independent parish church. *Oliver de Tracy, Rector*

1272 EDWARD I

1307 EDWARD II

1327 EDWARD III

1332 Devon Lay Subsidy Roll

1347 - 50, and 1361 Black Death

1377 RICHARD II

1399 HENRY IV

1403 HENRY V

1422 HENRY VI

1461 EDWARD IV

1470 HENRY VI
Wars of the Roses

1471 EDWARD IV

1483 RICHARD III

1485 HENRY VII

1509 HENRY VIII who set up the Church of England

1547 EDWARD VI

1553 MARY Returned to church

Disagreement with Croyde about Tithes.
Sir Stephen Hyam, Rector

1294 Death of Sir Mauger de St Aubin, whose effigy is in the church.

1308 *Edmond de Knovyl, Rector*

1344 *Master William de Doune Rector*

1349 *Master John Dyrworth, Rector*

1361 *Sir Andrew de Tregors, Rector*

1374 *Sir John Hope, Rector*

1391 *John Lynnley, Rector*

1402 Chapel at South Hole licensed

1428 Thomas Haccombe held Ham and Pickwell at his death.

1433 *Master Martin Lercedyken, Rector*

1447 *Master Edward Leghe, Rector*

1450 *Sir Richard Row/Rouse, Rector*

1458 G'ham paid 11d to repair Barnstaple Bridge

1465 *William Slugge and Thomas Cutford, Rectors*

1499 *John Chaplyn, Rector*

1516 *John Gevons/Gebons, Rector*

1528 *John Holwyl/Holway, Rector*

1538 Georgeham Church Registers begin

1553 Four bells known to be in church

	of Rome		tower.
1558	ELIZABETH I	**1559**	*John Gread, Rector*
		1571	Plague in the village.
		1576	*William Culme, Rector*
1588	Spanish Armada		
1603	JAMES I	**1603**	John Newcombe of Pickwell died.
1625	CHARLES I		
		1630	Risdon and Westcote, historians of Devon.
		1631	Foote Farm existed
1632	Lay Subsidy		
		1638	*John Berry, Rector*
1649	COMMONWEALTH	**1649**	*William Pyke, Rector*
1660	CHARLES II		
		1660	*Thomas Colley, Rector.*
1665	Great Plague		
1666	Great Fire of London	**1666**	Date on Mill Farm, Croyde.
		1667	Chaloner's School, Braunton, buys land at Darracott.
1675	Ogilby's maps		
		1678	Date on Millies Cottage, Georgeham.
		1680	First chalice and paten given to church.
1685	JAMES II		
1689	WILLIAM and MARY		
		1690	'Sands Maps', showing Putsborough, Baggy.
		1692	First dated stone in churchyard
		1698	*Carew Hoblyn, Rector.*
1702	ANNE		
1714	GEORGE I		
		1721	Donn's maps
1727	GEORGE II	**1727**	Terrier of Georgeham Church.
		1728	Duke of Ripparda lands at Woolacombe
		1729	*William Marvin, Rector*
		1730	Deed no. A105
		1741	John Harris, Pickwell, MP for Barnstaple

1744 *George Drake, MA, Rector*

1748 Six bells made for tower

1750 *William Chichester, Rector*

1753 Dean Miles' Questionnaire

1754 John Harris, Pickwell, MP for Barnstaple

1760 GEORGE III

1762 Church restored (beautified)

1771 Land tax, information available for Georgeham

1771 *Henry Marker, George Sandford, Rectors*

1782 *Nathaniel Bridges, Rector*

1783 *Thomas Hole, Rector*

1792 Beginning of Wars with France

1794 Deed no. A106

1799 Wreck of HMS Weazle off Baggy. Rev. Thomas Hole buys part of foremast. Second chalice given to church.

1808 Deed no. A104

1809 First OS maps published, information available for Georgeham.

1815 End of wars with France (Napoleonic War)

1820 GEORGE IV

1822 Lysons' History of Devon.

1827 Greenwood's maps

1830 WILLIAM IV

1831 *Francis Hole, Rector*

1832 Tax returns

1833 Pickwell estate map

1836 Land given for Methodist Chapel in Georgeham, soon sold to Baptists.

1837 VICTORIA

1839/40 Tithe Maps

1840 Georgeham Tithe Map and Apportionments.

1851 Census

1861 Census

1871 Census

1881 Census

1891 Census

1894 Civil Parishes introduced

1901 EDWARD VII

Last available Census

1904/5 OS maps, second edition

1912 GEORGE V

1914 First World War

1936 GEORGE VI

1939 Second World War

1952 ELIZABETH II

1852 Gun recovered from the Weazle

1867 *William Chorley Lovebond, Rector*

1868 Bridge built over stream at Foote Farm

1869 *Thomas Hole, Rector*

1870 *Francis Hole, Rector*

1872 *William Genn Morcom, Rector.*

1874 Croyde church built

1876 Restoration of the church.

1881 *Robert Bibby de Wolf, Rector*

1883 New Baptist chapel built at Georgeham

Murder of PC Creech

Walter Eustace Cox MA, Rector.

1886 *William Henry George, Rector*

Francis Hole, Rector

1907 Rifle Range opened

1914 *Walter Matthew Parker, Rector.*

1921 *Alfred Rose, Rector*

1926 Bells restored, two added.

Church clock as War Memorial

Parish Institute opened

1930 *Algernon Edgar Worsley, Rector.*

1936 *Harry Sharples, Rector.*

1948 War memorial Screen in church

Women's Institute, Georgeham branch formed.

Mains water supply to village.

1957 *Fisher Ferguson MA, Rector.*

1959 Heddon Mill working

	John Manaton, Rector
1967	13th century font found in churchyard.
	John Reginald Jackson, Rector
1968	Gun recovered from wreck of HMS Weazle
1974	*Bernard John Bedford Carr, Rector.*
1977	Jubilee Year Village Fete, film still extant.
1978/9	Davids Hill houses built.
1988	*David Rudman, Rector.*
2000	Millennium Garden constructed
2001	Houses built on the Glebe Field.
2002	Brian Strange inducted as Priest in Charge.

Appendix 2: Sources

H Stevenson Balfour.	The History of Georgeham and Croyde. 1965 and 1989.
Lois Lamplugh.	A Book of Georgeham and the North West Corner of Devon 1995.
'Ben Gunn'	Tales of Old Woolacombe. 1999
Margaret Reed	Mortehoe and Woolacombe on the Record. 1997
Lois Lamplugh.	Barnstaple: Town on the Taw. 1983/2002
D J V Fisher	The Anglo-Saxon Age
Anthea Jones	A Thousand Years of the English Parish.
W G Hoskins	Devon
Tristram Risdon	Survey of the County of Devon. 1811 edition.
Thomas Westcote	A View of Devonshire
Charles Croslegh	Bradninch

Georgeham Tithe Map and Apportionments 1839, from the North Devon Records Office and from notes from the collection given by Mr and Mrs P Mounteney.

Georgeham Tax Returns, 1792 and 1832, from copies in the collection given by Mr and Mrs P Mounteney.

Georgeham Parish Records Information. As above

Extracts from Georgeham Parish magazine, 1907 - 1919. As above

Extracts from the Minutes of the Parish Institute, 1926 - 1944. As above.

Extracts from the early minutes of Georgeham Parish (Civil) Council. North Devon Records Office.

Appendix 3: Other Sources of Information About Georgeham

O J Reichel	Victoria History of Devon
O J Reichel	Hundreds of Devon
Lysons.	Devonshire
H Stevenson Balfour	The Weazle, paper from The Transactions of the Devonshire Association.
Rev. T Whale	Devonshire Extracts from the Pipe Rolls, Henry II, Richard I.
Sir William Pole (d 1635)	History of Devonshire, pub. 1791
William Marshall	The Rural Economy of the West of England

Devon Feet of Fines

Bishops'/Episcopal Registers, ed. Hingston Randolf (John de Grandison, Branscombe, Quivil)
North Devon Records Office.

Church Papers	W H Rogers' Transcription
Lay Subsidy Roll, 1332	North Devon Records Office
Book of Fees, 1244	North Devon Records Office

.North Devon Journal Herald, Aug 2nd, Nov. 8th and 15th, 1883.

Monthly Returns of the Georgeham Volunteers.

Deeds A 105,106 (1793), settling the Pickwell Estates. North Devon Records Office.

Milles/Miles Devon MSS, vol. 2. Bodlian Library

Diary of Captain Webber of Buckland.

Transactions of the Devonshire Association. Vol. 89 (Mesolithic sites), Vol. 39 (Church Plate), Vol. 24 (Defence)

Appendix 4: Illustrations Used in the Text

Index